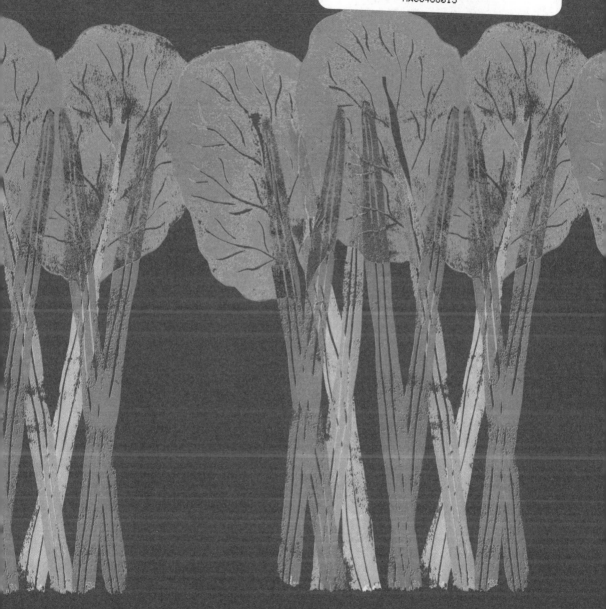

REKHA'S KITCHEN GARDEN

To Rajni, Dhirun, Riana, and Jaiden
for ALWAYS believing in me.

REKHA'S
KITCHEN GARDEN

Seasonal produce and homegrown wisdom
from a year in one gardener's plot

REKHA MISTRY

CONTENTS

Introduction 6–13

Purple sprouting broccoli
Lettuce
Radish
Spring cabbage
Spring onion
Carrot
Swiss chard
Parsley
Rhubarb

SPRING

14–53

Eggplant
Cucumber
Tomato
Chile
Sweet pepper
Green bean
Onion
Sweet corn
Zucchini
Basil
Garlic
Garden pea
Strawberry
Spinach
Dill
Potato
Chives
Cilantro
Mint
Beets

SUMMER
54–135

Apple
Raspberry
Florence fennel
Celeriac
Squash
Turnip

FALL
136–63

Kale
Savoy cabbage
Leek
Brussels sprouts
Parsnip

WINTER
164–87

Index 188–89
Acknowledgments 190–91
About the author 192

From a young age, growing up in Zambia, my mother's kitchen garden (vegetable plot) was my escape. Back then, I wasn't into "gardening" as such, and yet I loved to help her tend to her crops. As a child, this was my slice of paradise.

Then life happened. I grew up. Moved to a new country. Got married and started a family of our own. That was when my own green thumb sprouted. I wanted my children to understand where food on their plates came from, and—more importantly—the time it takes for vegetables to grow. I wanted them to know that their dinner didn't start life with the beep of a barcode in a supermarket.

Our small home vegetable patch and the children's flying footballs were a recipe for disaster, so I plucked up the courage and signed up for a rented plot of land known as an allotment—then considered a retiree's playground, although this didn't phase me. This is where my kitchen garden journey truly began.

I wasn't born with a silver garden fork in my hand. In the beginning, I was self-taught, learning along the way. I asked questions. I researched how I could grow food organically and sustainably. I scoured second-hand gardening books, picking up tips from these writers and experts.

Before long, my allotment became far more than a pastime. I said goodbye to a successful 25-year career, started my gardening blog, and discovered a love for photography. I enrolled in a diploma program in Horticulture, which led to work as a professional gardener in a prestigious London garden—and at the same time kick-started a career as a garden and food writer and TV host.

Now, my love for fresh produce has outgrown the paradise that was my mother's kitchen garden; it's outgrown that tiny space that doubled as a family football field. It has become a way for me to share my experiences, my expertise, and—more importantly—my love for all things grow-your-own. It has led, one way or another, to this book.

INTRODUCTION

GROWING ORGANICALLY

Before I could start dreaming of what I'd harvest from my London plot, I had to tame it and cultivate its clay soil. Inspired by the writings of Lawrence Hills, I wanted to transform my overgrown haven organically and sustainably, using what little I knew from books and listening to other plot-holders. The organic ethos is at the heart of my gardening, and each technique I adopted was a small step toward sustainability.

Homemade compost

Ordering compost to spread over all my beds would be both unsustainable and expensive, so instead, I make my own. When I started, I had just one cone-shaped bin. In went most of the annual weeds I cleared, although not the perennials; those, like invasive bindweed (*Convolvulus*), I disposed of at the green waste site. Now I have four bays, which produce enough compost for a quarter of the plot, while the rest of my allotment is enriched with green manure (see right).

Rainwater

Plants love water, particularly pure, untreated rainwater. Rain barrels are the best way to catch and store this precious, free resource, and mine collect rainwater via downspouts from both the shed and greenhouse roofs. Like most gardeners, I just wish I could store much more of it.

Organic fertilizers

While homemade compost improves the soil, organic fertilizers nourish the plants. Two of my go-to fertilizers are blood and bone meal and organic liquid seaweed, sold by most garden centers.

I also make my own feed, or "tea", which I give to my flowering and fruiting plants. It's so simple to make. Add enough nutrient-rich nettle tops or comfrey leaves to almost fill a bucket, weight them down with a brick, then top off with rainwater (*not* tap water). Cover with a lid, leave for six weeks, strain, and it's ready to use: just combine 1 part feed to 10 parts rainwater in a watering can and apply once a week once flowers start to form.

Green manure

Crops deplete the soil of nutrients, but green manure plants put the goodness back. In winter, I sow a green manure crop—field peas with deep roots, Italian rye grass, or phacelia—over any bare ground. The plants protect the soil, while their roots draw nutrients up into the leaves. Then, in spring, I dig over the top growth back into the soil, where the plants rot down, ready to feed my vegetable crops. I sow more green manure in summer: at this time, buckwheat is ideal for covering bare ground and suppressing weeds. No farm manure for me—just green manure.

Right I allow some of my green manure, *Phacelia tanacetifolia*, to flower at the edge of the bed, in order to attract pollinators.

Far right Comfrey 'Blocking 14' provides an excellent free source of plant food.

Below Cottage-style kitchen gardening is both productive and pleasing to the eye—a simple, effective way to create biodiversity in a small space.

Above, far left The scent of *Calendula officinalis* helps deter pests in the plot—and its petals make a welcome addition to salads.

Below, far left Slugs and snails are lured into the trap by the beer's aroma. They'll go to mollusc heaven with happy, full bellies—leaving my plants unscathed.

Left To deter pests from my brassicas, I protect them with netting, and grow *Phacelia* and *Knautia* nearby to attract beneficial predators.

Pest control

Even after pests destroyed some of my first crops, I've never used off-the-shelf pesticides, which contain chemicals that can harm beneficial insects. Instead, I encourage diversity by growing different flowers among the vegetables, which help attract predators for any would-be pests.

For slugs and snails, I sink a container into the soil, fill it with the cheapest beer in town—then cheer when I find molluscs floating on the surface.

To prevent cabbage white butterfly from laying eggs on my brassicas, I drape soft netting over canes topped with bottles, and secure it with tent stakes. Henry, my trusty hawk kite, takes care of the bigger flying pests—especially pigeons.

In summer, I water the greenhouse floor and leave out a bucket of water. This discourages spider mites, which love dry heat and hate humidity.

Preventing disease

Years of experience have taught me that good ventilation, whether outside or indoors, is the key to disease prevention. Dampness that persists on leaves and stems can encourage the spread of fungal spores, but leaving space between plants encourages good air circulation, movement, and water evaporation. When I water, I also aim the flow at the base of the plant, where it is needed, and avoid splashing the leaves.

Companion planting

Growing beneficial plants next to crops is a chemical-free method of attracting natural predators and controlling pests. Calendula flowers and foliage repel aphids, borage is a bee magnet, while herbs such as mint and chives not only add flavor to dishes but keep pests from attacking brassicas and carrots.

CROP ROTATION

Vegetables from the same family group are best grown together, but they also tend to suffer from the same pests and diseases. To prevent these from building up, I move each crop family to a different position in the plot each year. My system is very basic: I divide the long plot into four sections and allocate one to each group, as in the simple diagram below. I then move each group around the plot, and after four years it will be back in its original position. Legumes, for example, leave behind beneficial nitrogen, so I plant nitrogen-hungry brassicas where they grew. Potatoes always follow brassicas, while onions appreciate the crumbly soil of last year's potato bed.

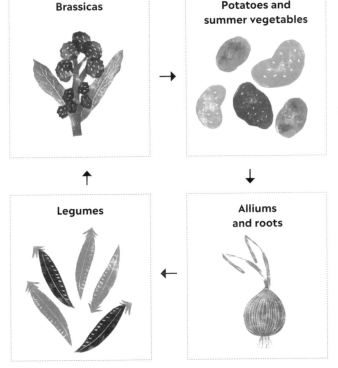

Brassicas

Potatoes and summer vegetables

Legumes

Alliums and roots

Brassicas include purple sprouting broccoli (PSB), spring and Savoy cabbages, turnips, kale, and Brussels sprouts.

In addition to potatoes, this includes tomatoes, zucchini, cucumbers, and outdoor zucchini varieties that don't need the greenhouse's heat.

Legumes include garden peas and green beans. I'll also plant corn and winter squash in this area.

Alongside alliums like onions, spring onions, leeks, and garlic, this plot includes roots like carrots, beets, and parsnips.

A YEAR IN THE PLOT

You won't find a garden notebook by my bedside, or shelves stuffed with gardening books. I'm one of those people who can hold information in my head, and that's where I keep my garden filing system. So how do I decide what to grow and where to grow it? After a year in the plot, I realized the best way to use the growing space and plan for the following year was to organize crops according to when they were harvested. I'm a true believer in cooking and eating seasonally, and that's why this book is organized by the time of year everything is most likely to be ready. Once I know this, I think backward, figuring out when I need to sow seeds, grow, and plant each crop outdoors.

In mid-fall, after I've brought in the last summer harvest and most crops are cleared away, I'm left with an almost-blank canvas. I'm not an artist, but I'd like to think I paint with plants as I start to plan next year's artwork, always with the crop-rotation plan (see p11) firmly etched in my mind.

ESSENTIAL TOOLS AND EQUIPMENT

Here's a look at a few of the tools that I use time and time again on the plot.

Sowing equipment

An electric heat mat, propagators, and coir pellets soaked in warm water are essential for crops started indoors early in the year, while over in the potting shed my "tidy tray" stops the potting mix I scoop into trays and pots from spilling everywhere. I firm the mix into containers with wooden tampers of different sizes, then sieve over a fine layer to achieve even germination of seeds. Large seeds, such as beans, peas, and sweet corn, are sown into Rootrainers, which are deep modules that encourage strong root systems.

Hardening off

Once the seedlings are repotted individually, using my trusted mini-dibble, they go into the cold frame. In this halfway house, they spend two weeks acclimatizing to conditions outdoors prior to planting outside. I also have horticultural fleece on hand to cover seedlings in case of an unforeseen heavy frost.

Planting and harvesting

A traditional wooden-handled fork is ideal for prepping the soil; a shovel-spade is used for making planting holes, and a good, sturdy rake creates a fine tilth (as well as earthing up potatoes). For weeding, nothing compares to my Hori-Hori knife, which I also use to make neat drills for quick sowing. Finally, when it comes to harvesting crops, I use pruners and snips, cleaning and sharpening both after every use.

MONTHLY TASKS IN MY PLOT

The chart below doesn't contain every single monthly job I undertake in the plot, but it does include many key tasks. It is intended as an overview to give you a good idea of what I do when, over the course of a whole year.

	At home & in the greenhouse	Outdoor
Jan	• Sow eggplant, chiles, and peppers (home). • Order seed potatoes. • Sort out seed packets; remove any that are out of date.	• Prune the apple tree. • Rake debris from around summer-fruiting raspberry canes. • Force rhubarb for an early harvest.
Feb	• Sow onions (greenhouse) and tomatoes (home). • Chit potatoes on a warm, bright windowsill.	• Plant bare-root fruit trees or shrubs. • Cut back fall-fruiting raspberry canes.
Mar	• Sow peas in deep root Rootrainers (greenhouse). • Prick out lettuce. • Clean and sanitize the greenhouse.	• Apply fertilizer and mulch around raspberry canes. • Turn in green manure. • Harvest the last parsnips (but leave some to flower).
Apr	• Sow squash, zucchini, and green beans. • Move tomato plants to the greenhouse.	• Plant first early seed potatoes outdoors, and spring cabbages—raised in the cold frame. • Prepare nettle and comfrey teas.
May	• Sow cucumbers (greenhouse). • Move eggplant, chile, and pepper plants into the greenhouse.	• Plant garlic, onion, and tomato plants outside. • Incorporate compost and straw into bean growing area, and erect bean poles. • Provide greenhouse shading.
Jun	• Give weak seaweed feed to eggplants, chiles, and peppers. • Pinch basil tips to encourage side shoots.	• Thin out beet rows. • Keep on top of weeding duties. • Earth-up maincrop potatoes and harvest early potatoes.
July	• Keep greenhouse doors and vents open. • Harvest first eggplants to promote further fruits.	• Pin down strawberry runners to create new plants. • Feed green beans with comfrey tea when in flower.
Aug	• Feed eggplants and peppers when flowers appear. • Wet the greenhouse floor to create humidity.	• Direct-sow winter radish. • Protect corn with netting as cobs start to form. • Harvest onions, then sow quick-growing green manure.
Sep	• Sow romaine lettuce and onions (cold frame). • Water during early mornings to prevent mildew.	• Remove leaves around winter squash to aid ripening. • Harvest last zucchini and midseason potatoes.
Oct	• Sow early peas (greenhouse). • Bring container-grown chard and mint under cover. • Wash, sanitize, and store greenhouse pots.	• Earth up leeks. • Stake Brussels sprouts. • Check netting on brassicas to keep out birds. • Weed and tidy around turnips. • Sow green manure.
Nov	• Plant garlic cloves in pots (greenhouse). • Ventilate greenhouse on mild days. • Clear yellowing and dead foliage to prevent disease.	• Sow chive seeds direct. • Harvest parsley and cover with cloches. • Gather fallen leaves from trees to make leafmold.
Dec	• Harvest fresh mint and romaine lettuce. • Check stored produce; discard any that has spoiled. • Gather seed catalogs, make wish lists, and place orders to avoid disappointment in spring.	• Plant out bare-root raspberry canes. • Harvest parsnips and Brussels sprouts. • Enjoy the brief silence of the dormant plot before the gardening year begins again next month

SPRING

Spring is a real mix. As the days start to lengthen, the crops that overwintered from last year can take a laid-back approach as they grow. For me, however, it's a race as I embark on a seed-sowing marathon.

PURPLE SPROUTING BROCCOLI

Brassica oleracea (Italica Group)

Every year, I say I won't grow purple sprouting broccoli (PSB). Sometimes, I am an impatient gardener and it just takes *so long*. PSB is a biennial, starting life in one year but only producing florets in the next. But the truth is, aside from its long growing season, PSB is a great crop that needs no more attention than, say, kale or Brussels sprouts. In fact, it bridges the gap between my sprouts and spring cabbage harvests. Unlike regular broccoli, this purple, multistemmed variety offers a bright pop of late-winter color at a time when the allotment is mostly dormant. And so I sow it, and come the following year, I'm glad. After months of harvesting all shades of green, seeing those purple spears tells me that spring—sunshine, warm soil, a new growing year—is about to begin.

Rekha's favorites

'Cardinal'
'Purplelicious'
'Purple Sprouting Early'

Sowing

Purple sprouting broccoli is a laid-back plant, and so I take a leaf out of its book (pardon the pun) and ignore the recommended sowing times of March and April. There's no point in rushing to get these seeds sown when there are so many other vegetables to sow, and so many seed trays taking up space in my greenhouse and cold frame. I much prefer to wait until early May, when most of my seedlings have been moved on. I'll sow a tiny pinch (no more than seven or eight) of these small seeds in a 2¾in (7cm) pot, then sieve over a light covering of seed-starting mix. After watering, I place the pot in the cold frame because the greenhouse is too warm and small containers can run dry within days.

Ironically, given its long growing period, PSB seed is quick to germinate. Within four weeks, the seedlings are ready to go into individual 2¾in (7cm) pots. Slugs are on the prowl and somehow squeeze into the cold frame, so I put traps on the ground inside it. These are large, empty yogurt cups cut down and filled with warm beer.

Planting outdoors

I like to plant my young PSB crop outside as summer begins, so that the plants can quickly take root and establish in the warm soil. So once I've repotted the seedlings and watered them, I set to work preparing the growing area by applying a layer of mulch—a mix of organic farmyard manure and homemade compost. PSB is happy growing in sun or partial shade.

Above Just 2–3 weeks after being repotted, the young PSB is ready for transplanting.

Below As soon as they germinate, the PSB seedlings show their distinctive, purple-colored stems.

Above Netting with a small mesh stops insects and bird pests from getting anywhere near my PSB plants. It is durable and also reusable.

Opposite Using sharp garden snips, I harvest PSB florets. with a good length of stalk and a couple of young leaves, which are also tasty.

Opposite, bottom When harvesting PSB, I always cut off the floret at the top of the main stem first. This encourages the side shoots below to produce further florets.

Around mid-June, I plant the PSB outside , setting each plant 12in (30cm) apart. This spacing might look excessive but the plants will soon grow taller, producing plenty of broad leaves to make the most of the summer sun. In the meantime, they need to be covered with netting to protect them from cabbage white butterfly (see p30), and from hungry pigeons. During summer, as the plants establish, I also water regularly (2.2 gallons/10 litres every fourth day), as well as giving them a weekly nitrogen-rich nettle feed (see p8).

By September, as the mornings turn cooler, the plants are tall enough to need staking with sturdy canes—just in case the high winds of fall and winter try to flatten them. I also cut right down on watering to harden the plants for the colder weather. After that, I can pretty much forget about the plants from October until February, when frost and sometimes snow further toughen up the plants. That being said, I do leave the netting in place, even in winter; pigeons love a broccoli snack no matter the time of year.

Harvesting

As winter turns to spring, the plants awaken and tender stems of purple florets soon appear on the main and side stems. These can be snipped off with a sharp knife or pruners. I keep coming back to each plant throughout March and April—the more I cut, the more floret-bearing stems emerge. Cropping continues right up until early May when the plants are finally exhausted.

Kitchen tip

After such a long wait, it would be an awful shame to boil these tender stems to death. Instead, I steam them for around 10 minutes. Meanwhile, I prepare a *bagna cauda* sauce by blending together lots of crushed garlic with mashed anchovies, butter, and olive oil. Cook in a pan over a low heat, then pour over the steamed PSB and serve with crusty bread. Simply delicious.

LETTUCE

Lactuca sativa

I remember the first time I grew lettuce. No seed trays, just a few 2¾in (7cm) pots leftover from some strawberry plants the year before. And the number of seed varieties to choose from! Having never seen such a wide range of lettuce varieties in the supermarket, discovering the options available to grow left my jaw wide open. I couldn't believe how much more there was to try beyond the usual iceberg lettuce and bags of limp lettuce leaves.

Main sowing

If I wanted to, I could kick-start my lettuce-growing season in January. Why? Because lettuce will germinate even in temperatures as low as 36°F (2°C). But I resist, keeping this month purely for sowing chiles, peppers, and eggplants. I prefer to save lettuce for February, when I sow my first few seeds.

Lettuce seed isn't fussy about the container it's sown in, as long as there are drainage holes. In February, I scatter the seed over a 2in– (5cm–) thick layer of seed starting mix

Rekha's favorites

'Marvel of Four Seasons' (Butterhead)
'Oriental Mix' (Baby leaf)
'Parris Island Cos' (Romaine)
'Oakleaf Green' (Loose-leaf)

and then sieve another thin layer of mix over the top. Sow thinly, otherwise by harvest time you'll be eating nothing but salad for weeks. Then, either water from the base (see p98), or use a can fitted with a fine rose to avoid seed displacement. Once soaked, the containers can be set aside in an unheated greenhouse or a cold frame.

After this first February sowing, I continue to sow a few seeds every month (successional sowing), then stop around July because lettuce seed won't germinate when night-time temperatures are above 59°F (15°C). My winter-sown seedlings will begin to emerge within 3–5 days, and around two weeks later they're ready to transfer into module trays. Modules allow the roots to spread and take up sufficient nutrients, rather than fight for space and food in a seed tray. I water until it seeps from the base of the pots, then allow them to drain.

Planting outside

By early April, my first lettuce seedlings are ready to be planted outdoors, but I keep some horticultural fleece on

Garden tip

Mix up your lettuce crop by sowing different varieties from month to month. I particularly love loose-leaf cut-and-come-again mixes, which I sow into a large container that I keep in the greenhouse. These are ready to harvest in as little as 10 days, with no thinning or repotting needed—and as the name suggests, new leaves appear once the top growth is cut away. I usually get about four harvests from a single plant before the leaves grow too old and bitter to eat.

Far left I use a small dibble and gently uproot the fragile lettuce seedlings

Left When plucking out into individual modules, always hold the seedling by the leaves, not the stem.

Above Lettuces are ideal for repurposed containers, such as this old wheelbarrow, as long as there are drainage holes.

Centre A month after repotting, lettuce plants have good root systems and can be planted outdoors.

Right After watering, the young lettuce leaves are out of the reach of ground-dwelling slugs.

Garden tip

Lettuce is a great crop for succession sowing. This means regularly sowing a few seeds to produce a continuous supply. With lettuce seed, I like to sow a new batch every 3–4 weeks.

hand, ready to cover the crop if a late frost is forecast. First I hand-weed the area, then rake in a little organic fertilizer. To save space, I plant my first seedlings a little closer together than the 6in (15cm) that seed packets usually advise. In two weeks' time I will thin them out to the recommended spacing, allowing better air circulation around the plants I want to keep growing. The thinnings aren't wasted because I replant these to give an extra crop. Never pack lettuce plants in too tightly or the leaves will be at risk of succumbing to a fungal disease called grey mold (see p43).

As the spring sunshine warms the soil, it awakens not only weed seeds but also hibernating—and hungry—molluscs. Once I've planted my young lettuce seedlings and watered them, I make sure to place a beer trap (see p10) close to the area. I then cover my newly planted seedlings with a cloche, to protect the leaves from any unexpected overnight frosts. These remain in place day and night to speed up growth. By May, when temperatures are warmer, the cloches are gathered up and stored away until fall, when they are brought out again to cover lettuce still growing outdoors. Lettuce needs to be kept well-watered and weeded; it hates neglect.

Fall sowing

In September, I transition to sowing romaine lettuces, which are hardy to very low temperatures. The seedlings will begin to emerge within 3–5 days, and within around two weeks, they're ready to repot. Because I plan to grow these plants in the greenhouse, I transfer them to pots or troughs that are at least 2 pints (1 liter) in volume. They'll continue to grow in the greenhouse, sheltered from the winter weather conditions outdoors.

Harvesting

The joy of home-grown lettuce is how quickly the harvest comes around. Even in the early stages, I make the most of any surplus seedlings I don't transfer into module trays, by washing and then adding them whole to my salad bowl.

The real harvest starts around four weeks after planting outdoors—meaning that my first, February-sown butterhead crop will be ready around May. Depending on what I need, I'll either harvest a whole head, or take just a few outer leaves when needed, leaving the rest to stay fresh in the ground for the next time.

The perfect partner: Garlic

When I first grew lettuce, my plants were attacked by aphids—even outdoors where air movement should have disturbed the insects. Then I learned how the strong scent of garlic (see pp100–103) can help deter aphids when planted nearby. It's a harmonious pairing: the garlic keeps the lettuce healthy, while the quick-growing lettuce is harvested before its roots can impede the garlic's growth.

Far left Butterhead and loose-leaved lettuces are ready to pick just a month after planting.

Left When harvesting a whole lettuce, leave the roots attached and it will keep for longer.

23

RADISH

Raphanus sativus

Spring radishes are my least favorite vegetable. I just cannot stand the raw, spicy mustard smell that shoots up the nostrils. But do I grow them? Yes, because my family loves them. And given that you can harvest them within a month of sowing, they are one of the quickest vegetables to grow and ideal for getting young children hooked on vegetable gardening. Radishes aren't space divas, either, and are happy in small pots or between rows of onions or other crops. Below, I describe how I grow spring radishes, and I've also included a note on winter varieties like 'Daikon' on p26, which I do happen to love.

Rekha's favorites

Spring varieties
'Felicia'
'French Breakfast'
Winter varieties
'Black Spanish'
'Daikon'

Sowing under cover
Over the years, I've learned a thing or two about growing spring radishes. First, although they aren't frost hardy, they can germinate in soil temperatures as low as 41°F (5°C). This means I can start them off in early March as long as I sow under cover, either in my greenhouse or under a cloche. Second, radishes absolutely hate root

24

disturbance, so I don't use seed trays. Transplanting the seedlings could shock and even kill them. Instead, I sow my first few radish seeds of the season into 5in (13cm) terracotta pots, each containing moist seed-starting mix that I've tamped down. I space the seeds at least ¾in (2cm) apart, then sieve over a 1cm (½in) layer of mix. They're then given a good watering and kept in the greenhouse to trigger germination.

Even though radishes don't mind the cold and are being kept under cover, I'll place horticultural fleece over the emerging seedlings at the end of each day, to protect them from sudden, sharp overnight temperature drops. The UK's weather is unpredictable at best, and at this time of year, anything is possible—I've seen snow fall on my London allotment in April, so I take no chances.

Sowing outdoors

Like lettuce, radishes are perfect for succession sowing (see p22), and every month or thereabouts, I'll sow a few more seeds to keep up a regular radish supply for my family. Once the risk of frost has passed (usually around mid-May), I'll do this outside.

Before each sowing, I make sure that the planting area is ready. When it comes to moisture, these roots can be little

Above Always firm the mix when sowing to remove any air pockets.

Center Radish seed is large enough to pick up and sow individually.

Right I use a small can with a fine rose so seeds aren't displaced when watering.

Below After germination, I thin the seeds to leave enough space between each for the swelling roots.

attention-seekers (see below), so I choose a spot in partial shade and with good drainage, then work in a fair amount of well-rotted manure. I then create a shallow drill with my finger, around ½in (1cm) deep and 6in (15cm) long. I'll scatter a small amount of seed along this drill, water it in, and leave it to germinate. Within 7–10 days, I am thinning out seedlings, pulling out the weaker ones to leave around 1¼in (3cm) between each remaining plant.

Because they are small and fast-growing, radishes are perfect for intercropping (sowing or planting between other crops). They work well with slow-growing crops such as parsnips, or between rows of onions because the radishes will have been harvested long before the bulbs swell. When I'm sowing my peas, I also like to incorporate a few radish seeds. Before the pea plants reach 6in (15cm), the family will be munching fresh radishes.

Growing and harvesting

In the short window between sowing and harvesting, it's vital that the mix or soil be kept moist. If radishes suffer any form of drought, on account of an unexpectedly hot day or me neglecting my watering duties, they'll quickly throw a fit and "bolt" (produce a flower stalk), which leaves the root inedible.

The telltale sign that radishes are ready to harvest is when their swollen roots can be seen sitting a little above the soil. They are easily lifted by hand with a gentle pull; no fork needed. I've even mastered the knack of lifting a radish and brushing away loose soil in one quick action.

Winter radishes

Also called mooli, these are much bigger than spring types as well as hardier. White 'Daikon' is my favorite, and although it can be sown in spring, I've found this variety (and 'Black Spanish') performs better sown in late summer for a fall crop.

I sow seeds (exactly as I sow outdoor spring radishes) around the end of August, while the soil is still warm. These seeds are larger, so I space them 2in (5cm) apart. Within two weeks, when they have produced a pair of true leaves, I thin them to 4in (10cm) apart. 'Daikon' is a big, long root while 'Spanish Black' has a healthy girth, so both need plenty of space. I keep the soil consistently moist, and by the end of October the tops are jutting out of the soil, ready to harvest.

Top 'Black Spanish', a round winter radish, has crisp, white flesh.

Center Pick radishes as you need them by grasping the base of the leaves and pulling gently.

Right Sow seeds of different radish varieties and you'll have a fantastic range of both colors and shapes.

SPRING CABBAGE

Brassica oleracea (Capitata Group)

Before growing my own cabbage, I would turn up my nose at those densely packed balls of blanched leaves in the supermarket. Back then, they were sold wrapped in thick cellophane, and the foul smell that emerged when I cut open the wrap was enough to put *me* off, let alone the family. I had to wash the shredded leaves in vinegar before cooking them to mask the odor. Then I grew my own, and discovered what a marvels cabbage can be: its broad, deep-green leaves, veined and textured with a waxy sheen that lets water droplets slide off them. The unfurling of pointy cabbage leaves from their tightly formed hearts marks a shift in the seasons, as the last of the winter vegetables are harvested and the first days of spring arrive. And the taste! I remember using the word "sweet" when I cooked our first cabbage. It felt revolutionary.

Rekha's favorites

'Greyhound' (Hispi variety)
'Primo'
'Spring Hero'

Sowing and thinning

Spring cabbage starts life in November. Seed module trays are my go-to container for this crop: I fill each tray with seed starting mix, firm it in, and then sow three

seeds into each module before sieving another ½in (1cm) layer of mix over the top. The trays are then watered from the base (see p98) and left in the greenhouse. At this time of the year, moisture evaporation is minimal, so I only water again if the mix is dry more than halfway down the module. I check this by inserting a thin bamboo stick down the side of the tray, a bit like checking the oil level on a vehicle.

After about a week, the seedlings emerge. I immediately thin out the two weaker-looking seedlings from each module, leaving the strongest one to continue growing until four true leaves form. This takes around four weeks from sowing. I then repot the seedlings into 2¾in (7cm) containers filled with potting mix, water them, and leave them in the greenhouse to grow. As the weather cools, growth slows down and the plants go slightly dormant. At this time of year, I water only if the mix feels slightly dry when I stick my finger down the side of the pot.

Planting outside

I plant my cabbage outdoors in early March, but the process starts two weeks before that, as the young plants need to be hardened off first (see p12). All they have known is the cozy greenhouse; to be planted directly outside would shock them. As a halfway house, in late February I move the pots into my cold frame—a boxlike structure with a lid but without a base. Mine has glass panes in an aluminum frame and a hinged lid that I can prop open. Once inside, the plants can gradually acclimatize to outdoor conditions before being planted.

After two weeks have passed, I add well-rotted garden compost to the planting area, then firm it down with my feet (heel-toe, heel-toe) to remove any air pockets. Finally, I rake in a handful of cabbage fertilizer. For each plant, I dig a hole deep enough to hold the rootball, so that the first set of true leaves sits in line with the soil's surface, before firming the plant in well. The recommended spacing on

Top Sieve mix over such fine seeds to give just a light covering.

Above After thinning to one seedling per module, the second pair of true cabbage leaves starts to form.

Above Spaced fairly close together, spring cabbages produce small heads that are the perfect size for a meal.

Opposite right and bottom From late May, Hispi cabbages have formed good hearts and are ready to cut. Before I take them home, the tough outer leaves are removed and go straight onto the compost heap.

the seed packet would result in large cabbage plants; however I prefer smaller ones, so I leave just 8in (20cm) between plants.

Once my cabbages are planted, I water at the base, then set a few beer traps for my slug buddies (see p10), before securing netting around the cloche frame. The netting deters two pests: pigeons and cabbage white butterfly, which could destroy a crop that I've spent the last four months caring for. From late spring to late summer, the butterflies lay their eggs on the underside of cabbage leaves, which the resulting caterpillars then eat their way through. These butterflies can have three life cycles in a single growing season; by laying netting as soon as I plant my crop, I'm doing everything I can to minimize the risk of an attack before their first life cycle begins.

Cabbages are hungry, thirsty plants. By adding compost and fertilizer before planting, I've given them plenty of food, and I water every other day as the weather warms in spring. Underwatering can stress the plants, which may bolt (flower) and turn the leaves bitter and inedible.

Harvesting

After all this hard work, I can sit back as spring progresses and watch the hearts of my cabbages start to form. Six weeks after planting outside, I check on the hearts, cupping my hands around them to feel the tightness of the folded leaves. Slugs may be happy to see the cabbages too, so while I water I check for slug damage and top off the beer traps if needed.

Some years, I've harvested cabbages as soon as early May. In my defense, the plants were definitely giving out "eat me now" vibes! But if I can wait, the cabbages should be ready around nine weeks after planting, or six months after sowing—typically late May or early June. Loppers in hand, I get to work and the sound of the stems being cut sends my brain into overdrive as I start to imagine the dishes I'll create with my cabbage harvest.

Kitchen tip

I can still recall the day I placed a cabbage on my late mother-in-law's table, and the look on her face as she decided what she would make with it. Her specialty was *muthiya,* a spicy dish of steamed cabbage balls ("muthi" means "to hold a clenched fist"). Flour, spices, shredded cabbage, sliced onions, and chopped cilantro come together with a splash of water and oil into a dough that is formed into dumpling-sized balls. It's a humble dish, but the puff of evocative steam it gives off when ready makes me glad that I watched and listened. Thanks, Mum.

GREEN ONION

Allium cepa

Green onions aren't fussy. They're comfortable growing in even the smallest of spaces, be that indoors on our bright kitchen windowsill or outside on the windy plot. Despite the name, they can also be grown all year round, even in the depths of winter. If my green thumbs get the urge to sow seeds in January, I can start off a few green onions in a pot in the greenhouse, then know full well that they'll germinate—albeit at a slower rate than at other times of year. They don't have a set harvest window: they can be picked as young as four weeks old, to be used like chives in a potato salad, or at 12 weeks, when I make a version of tabbouleh. Rather than use lots of parsley and mint, I'll add equal amounts of spring onion and parsley with diced radishes for crunch. By 20 weeks, I'll add them, diced, to chickpea flour batter to make savory gluten-free pancakes. Even if left to bolt, the seeds are edible—and are delicious added to my homemade naan.

Rekha's favorites

'Lilia'
'North Holland Bloodred'
'Purplette'
'Redmate'
'White Lisbon'

Sowing

As I've mentioned, my winter-sown green onion seed goes into containers—I use 5-pint (3-liter) pots. As the temperature in the greenhouse is warm, not hot, watering is kept to a minimum. Sometimes, even when the top looks dry, there may still be enough moisture in the potting mix, so I water only if it still feels dry when I insert my finger more than halfway down the side of the pot. Overwatering or allowing the mix to remain soggy can deprive the roots of air and may lead to plants dying prematurely. Apart from checking on moisture, the green onions need no more attention until I'm ready to harvest.

From March onward, I prefer to sow directly outdoors. There's no need to bother with module trays or seed pots: in spring, these are a precious resource as I race to sow as many other seed varieties as I can. Instead, I prepare the area where I plan to sow carrots (see

Far right In the warmth of the greenhouse, the January-sown green onions have put on growth in just four weeks.

Right These direct-sown green onions have been in the ground for almost eight weeks and are ready to pick.

pp36-39), raking the soil to achieve a good, even "crumb." While it may sound like a lot of work, this effort helps the green onion seed sit evenly, without getting lost deep beneath clods of soil, and this helps ensure uniform germination.

As I prepare the short drills for carrots, I sow green onion seeds in ½in- (1cm-) deep rows on either side of the drills. This lessens the chance of disturbing the carrot seeds or seedlings later. I then cover the spring onion drills over with soil, gently tamping it down to make good contact. Finally, with a fine rose attached to my watering can, I carefully water the newly sown area.

While the spring sun warms the soil, germination times can vary from 5-12 days, depending on how stubborn the seeds decide to be. As one row germinates, I think about sowing the next. Sowing rows between my carrots every three weeks until the end of August will give me plenty of green onions right up until the first frosts in November.

Harvesting

I usually start harvesting green onions when they are around eight weeks old, picking one or two from the row at 2in (5cm) intervals. Green onions don't need thinning, and harvesting them in this way leaves room for the rest to grow. After lifting the bulbs with a gentle tug of their slender, pungent stems, I gently remove excess soil before taking them home.

Right A row of green onions creates a strong-smelling barrier that keeps the root fly away from young carrot foliage (see p38).

Garden tip

Don't trim the roots when you harvest your green onions—they help keep the crop fresh. Put them in a jar with a little water for a couple of days instead of in the fridge.

Above and top
Holding my
pot-grown green
onions by the stem,
I harvest three or
four at a time and
leave the rest to
keep growing.

Left Try not to
damage the roots
when you pull up
direct-sown green
onions, then gently
remove any soil. Your
onions will stay fresh
for longer (see
Garden Tip).

35

CARROT

Daucus carota

The first time I successfully harvested my own carrots, I thought I'd moved up into some new echelon of the gardening world—not least because it had taken me five years. "No chance," said neighboring plot holders when I told them I was growing carrots, before explaining they are one of the hardest vegetables to grow because they end up riddled with carrot root fly maggots. I ignored their advice. What could possibly go wrong? You guessed it. My whole harvest became infested with carrot root fly.

It took another three years to find solutions that worked for me. The key was timing: knowing when to sow, when to thin, and even when to water to minimize pest attack. My research paid off and I now grow healthy, organic carrots.

Rekha's favorites

'Early Nantes 2'
'Lunar White'
'Red Samurai'
'Solar Yellow'
'Touchon'

Sowing

Carrots grow best in soil that isn't rich, and the area where my winter squashes were growing is ideal. I dig over the ground lightly, then incorporate some horticultural sand, which dilutes any remaining richness in the soil as well as producing a light, open texture. This allows the carrot roots to penetrate the earth and grow straight. Wonky carrots are usually caused by lumpy soil.

I sow my carrot seed in early March. The day before sowing, I rake back and forth then water the area using a can with a fine rose. Finally, I spread horticultural fleece over the surface to maintain soil heat. The scene is set.

The next morning, I move the fleece to one side and make three or five shallow drills, ½in (1cm) deep, spaced 2in (5cm) apart. I keep these short, no more than 12in (30cm), so there is room for two or three varieties along a single row measuring just under 39in (1m) in length. I then sow green onion and carrot seed alternately, always starting and ending with green onion drills (see "Perfect partner"). The pungent scent of the onion will help mask the smell of carrot foliage, which is what attracts the carrot root fly. After sowing, I gently knock soil over the seed to backfill the drill, then gently tamp down the soil to encourage the seed to make good contact. Once all my seed is sown, I water it, again using a can with a fine rose.

Finally, I re-cover the area with horticultural fleece. This helps raise soil temperature, hastening the germination process. As soon as the seed has germinated, I'll remove the fleece, only to replace it with Enviromesh. This very fine netting allows light through, but not carrot root fly or other pests. I recently bought "beach-windbreak style" Enviromesh with prestitched sections for canes. Once I've inserted the canes, I secure them in the soil to create a perimeter fence around my rows. The top of the mesh sits above the height range of the low-flying female carrot root flies and my plants are well protected. I'll also set a few beer traps (see p10), since slugs love carrot seedlings almost as much as the carrot root fly does!

As the days begin to warm, I take further precaution against carrot root fly by watering in the late evenings. When dusk falls, there are fewer flies on the wing and they have also become docile. This timing minimizes the risk of attack.

Above There's no way you could sow individual carrot seeds: they are tiny.

Below My Japanese hori hori (soil knife) is perfect for making shallow drills, and the stringline ensures the row is straight.

Garden tip

Getting to know the life cycle of a pest tells you when it is prevalent. Carrot root fly is first active from mid-May to June, so I sow in March and thin my crop before mid-May. The fly's second cycle is from August to September. Luckily, my June-sown carrot seed germinates quickly in the warmth and thinning is completed before August. Minimal disturbance will result in better crops.

Below Sow a "hedge" of green onions on either side of carrot plants for chemical-free pest control.

Thinning

Two weeks after germination, once the first true leaves have established, I start to thin out the carrot seedlings. As with watering, I carry out the thinning process at dusk when the carrot root fly is less active. I carefully thin out seedlings, leaving a space of 2in (5cm) between each when growing my favorite variety, 'Touchon'. These produce large roots, so I will thin out just once and not disturb the crop any further.

Harvesting

Seed packets usually advise you to harvest carrots 12 to 16 weeks after germination. However, I like to do a test harvest as early as 10 weeks, around mid-May, gently teasing one or two carrots out to see if I'm happy with the size. If not, I'll leave the rest to continue growing, even beyond the recommended date. As I've learned, these dates are just that: recommendations. They are not set in stone. In some years, I've had a harvest after 10 weeks; in others, my carrots have dragged their heels and I've waited until early June for a crop. I harvest with a little push followed by a little pull to release the root, then just brush off the soil with my hands.

I'll sow carrots again in June, never in the same place as the spring ones but, apart from not needing to use Enviromesh, I follow the same process. These will be harvested from fall onward. With carrots that are still in the ground, I cut off the foliage then cover the row with a thick mulch of straw, topped with black plastic. Over winter I harvest the roots as needed.

Perfect partner: Green onion

The female carrot root fly is deterred from laying eggs near my carrots by the strong aroma of green onion foliage (see p34). As well as using mesh, I sow carrot and green onion seed in alternate rows, ensuring green onion is on the outside to form an additional defensive barrier.

Left These just-harvested carrots have straight roots with no sign of pest damage.

Far left In early June, while harvesting the first of the March-sown carrots, I stand on a plank to spread my weight and avoid compacting the soil.

Below I love to grow different-colored heirloom carrots. They taste just as good as regular orange types.

Kitchen tip

Carrot cake is my go-to recipe when I've had a good harvest. That being said, I cannot resist the simple treat of tossing carrot sticks in sunflower oil, a dash of soy sauce, and a pinch of paprika. Roasted on high heat for 30 minutes until golden brown, the results are utterly delicious.

SWISS CHARD

Beta *vulgaris* subsp. *cicla* var. *flavescens*

I love Swiss chard. I hadn't encountered this leafy Casanova before I came to this country, but when I did, I quickly fell for it. Sometimes I wonder what my regular spinach would say about Swiss chard if it could talk: maybe "What the hell does that plant think it's doing, swaying those glossy leaves around like that?!" I sense the spinach might be jealous, especially of those long, colorful stems. It shouldn't worry, though. For me, both spinach (see pp112–15) and Swiss chard have a special place in the garden, and in the kitchen, too.

Sowing

Have you ever seen a Swiss chard seed? It's a fascinating little thing and I remember sowing chard for the first time one March. I scattered a few seeds over a firm bed of seed starting mix in a seed tray, covered them with a further ½in (1cm) of mix, then left the seeds for about a week to germinate. When I returned, I was shocked to find three, four, even five seedlings emerging from where I'd sown

Rekha's favorites

'Arancia'
'Fordhook Giant'
'Rhubarb'

42

Garden tip

Watch out for gray mold (botrytis), an airborne fungal disease that can spread quickly, especially in greenhouses and other enclosed, humid spaces. To reduce the risk, don't oversow into seed trays, as poor air circulation between crowded seedlings is an open invitation for disease to strike. I also keep my greenhouse well ventilated from spring onward, by leaving the door open during the daytime.

each seed. I thought, "Girl, did you oversow?!" After doing some research, I discovered that each chard "seed" is actually a cluster of several seeds. Now, every March I sow only 20 seed clusters, making sure they are evenly spaced in the seed tray. This lessens the problem of fungal diseases developing later when seedlings germinate and become overcrowded (see right).

Above To separate chard seeds before sowing them into modules, I use a wooden chopstick.

Below Red and yellow stems of young rainbow chard add color to the cold frame in mid-April.

Thinning and hardening off

Once my seedlings have germinated (usually after a week to 10 days), I thin them out. Leaving just one from each cluster to grow ensures the remainder have sufficient room, and I don't waste the thinned seedlings, which I add to salads. About five weeks after sowing, the seedlings have 2–4 true leaves, telling me it's time to repot them into 2¼ in (7cm) pots filled with peat-free potting mix. I give them a good watering, then move them into the cold frame for two weeks to harden off.

Planting outside

As the plot wakes up in spring, so do the weeds and the pests. In preparation for planting outdoors, I keep the growing area well weeded, and set beer traps for slugs (see p10) at the first sign of slime trails and poop piles.

Above Hardened-off chard is planted outside in late April. I firm it in well to anchor the roots before the stems grow tall.

Centre Picking just one or two colorful stems from each plant at a time ensures a steady supply.

Right With its vibrant veins and stems, chard is worthy of any garden, not just a vegetable garden.

Far right I don't always use pruners to harvest Swiss chard. The stems are easily twisted off from the base.

Swiss chard isn't a fussy plant and will grow well in full sun or partial shade, as long as it's sheltered from the wind. I plant mine in the brassica bed, alongside Brussels sprouts and kale. Too much rocking by the wind can result in premature bolting—although I've found that even this isn't too much of an issue. Simply chop off the flower stalk and the plant, none the wiser, will continue to grow.

Around seven weeks after sowing, toward the end of April, the hardened-off Swiss chard plants are ready to plant outside. Space them 12in (30cm) apart, to give them plenty of growing space and good air circulation both above and below ground. Finally, settle the plants into their new homes by giving them a good watering in. By early summer, the plants should be growing well. Meanwhile, I'm on pest patrol, as Swiss chard (along with spinach, beets, and other leafy crops) can fall prey to spinach leaf miner. Watch out for random blotch marks

on leaves, or leaves shriveling and turning brown: signs that maggots are feasting below the leaf surface. At the first sign, snip off all affected leaves and burn them to prevent the maggots from moving onto other plants.

Harvesting

Full-sized leaves and stems will be ready for picking around 15 weeks after sowing. To ensure a long harvest from my few maturing plants, as well as to keep them producing, I've found the best approach is to pick little and often. The quickest method of harvesting is to simply twist one or two stems off from the base. Later, when I'm weeding, I'll use a pair of snips to tidy up the plants and trim off any jagged edges or untidy stubs. The beauty of growing Swiss chard is that as long as you don't harvest too much at once, you can pick fresh stems right up until the first hard frost.

Kitchen tip

A Swiss chard harvest does double duty in the kitchen. For chard pinwheels, I liberally spread spicy, gluten-free chili paste over the leaves, roll them up tightly, and fit them into a steamer basket. Half an hour later, the steamed rolls can be cut into disks and enjoyed with a cup of masala chai. As for those crisp, colorful stalks, I'll chop them up and toss them in vinegar. This quick refrigerated pickle is the perfect accompaniment to a Friday night curry.

PARSLEY

Petroselinum crispum

When I was younger, I used to think that the sole use of parsley leaves was to garnish a cooked dish. Oh, how wrong I was! A fresh sprinkling of flat-leaf parsley with its light, mellow taste can lift a summer meal. And the slightly thicker, kalelike leaves of curly parsley can lend a depth of flavor when added early to slow-cooked dishes. Both varieties provide fresh leaves over a long growing season, making parsley a must-have herb in my kitchen garden!

Sowing

By early April, there isn't space in my greenhouse (or my cold frame, for that matter) to squeeze in yet another seed tray, so I'll often start my parsley off at home. By this point all my seed and module trays are full of other vegetable seedlings, so I use 2¾in (7cm) pots. Sowing just 3–4 seeds into each will give the seedlings enough space and prevent overcrowding. After watering I cover the pot with a plastic bag (remember, all my propagator lids are also in use) to create and conserve humidity. The covered

Rekha's favorites

'Lisette'
'Plain Leaf'

pots of parsley then sit on my sunny kitchen windowsill.

Parsley seeds need warmth and enough time—sometimes as long as three weeks—to kick-start their germination. This really tries my patience, but as soon as it happens, I take off the plastic bag and leave the plants to grow. Come July, I'll sow more parsley seed, this time direct into the warm soil of my allotment. These summer-sown seeds are sure to germinate within days.

Thinning and harvesting

Supposedly, parsley seedlings should be thinned out two weeks after germination, but I leave them to grow. Only after about eight weeks, when I notice that the seedlings are fighting for growing space, do I thin out the weaker ones. By this time, all the seedlings should have around 5–6 true leaves, so thinnings can be used in the kitchen.

Whether I've grown them indoors in pots or sown direct outdoors, when the true leaves appear it's hard to resist the urge to pick the fresh foliage. But I hold back. The plants are putting on growth both above and below the potting mix and would have to work twice as hard if I pinched off their leaves. Only when the foliage is much bushier do I start harvesting. The flavor of the fresh leaves is so much more intense than fast-grown, overfed supermarket parsley, and you don't need to take much—a few homegrown parsley leaves can go a long way.

Above Curly-leaf parsley, although not perennial, will grow through the year. It's the ideal indoor herb for winter.

Below Just a few freshly picked stems of flat-leaf parsley add fantastic flavor to summer dishes.

Kitchen tip

By early summer, I often have a glut of fresh herbs. To avoid waste, I chop up excess parsley leaves—along with rosemary, chives, mint, and fennel fronds—and mix them into butter, before forming them into discs and freezing. Melt the discs over new potatoes or make an herby omelette in the depths of winter. The memory of summer will come flooding back with every mouthful.

RHUBARB

Rheum x hybridum

Our family used to categorically hate rhubarb. Yes, I know "hate" is a strong word, but that really was the truth. Mind you, the rhubarb we hated was always store-bought, limp, and flavorless. For that reason, I never intended to grow my own. So imagine my shock, the first time I arrived to inspect my new allotment plot, when I discovered quite a few established rhubarb crowns! "Get rid of them," my family said (in unison). But I was curious. I decided to grow it for a year, and to cook with the results. If we still didn't like rhubarb, I would gladly uproot the plants and pass the crowns on to someone else.

That was 2012 and rhubarb still grows on my plot. Thanks to my famous Rhubarb cake (see p51), the crowns were saved and now we all look forward to rhubarb season.

Rekha's favorites

'Fulton's Strawberry Surprise'
'Timperley Early'
'Victoria'

Preparation and planting

Like many allotment gardeners, I inherited my rhubarb patch. These perennials develop new offshoot crowns annually, as older crowns die back. If you want to start a rhubarb patch from scratch, I'd advise doing so during winter, when the crowns are dormant and sold cheaply bare-root. Sure, I could buy an established plant in early summer, but they would cost a lot more—and either way, the stems can't be harvested in their first year, as this would only stress the plant while it establishes itself.

Rhubarb grows best in partial shade, and mine, although in the correct position, was right next to the soft fruit, which it was dominating. This rhubarb, a fantastic variety called 'Timperley Early', clearly needed its own dedicated section. I waited until November, after the plants had shed their leaves and gone dormant, then prepared a new patch beside the compost bins where the plants would enjoy some shade. The area was just 10¾sq ft (1 sq meter) in size, yet it took a good half hour to dig and loosen the soil—and that was before I worked in two large sacks of manure.

Whether planting new crowns or lifting and transplanting, the key is to make sure that the crown of the plant (the center, where new shoots emerge), sits slightly above soil level. Firm in well so the roots make good contact with the soil and to remove any air pockets. Water in (don't drench the plants), then leave them be.

Above In spring, when rhubarb appears above ground, I give the crown a generous mulch of manure mixed with straw.

Routine care

Rhubarb plants are hungry—that's why I worked in so much manure—and they are also thirsty. As soon as they wake in spring, I'll keep an eye on the moisture content in the soil, especially when temperatures rise. Around midsummer each year, I heap plenty of straw around the base of the crowns to help water percolate slowly down to the roots as well as reduce evaporation from the surface of the soil. They still need watering—usually twice a week, or more often during periods of intense heat—but the straw makes a noticeable difference.

The first year is all about caring for the patch—remember, no harvesting stems while the plants work to

establish strong root systems. Just keep your plants well-watered and tidy, removing leaves as soon as they die back to improve air circulation and reduce the chances of pest infestation or disease.

Forcing and harvesting

I took the first stems from my rhubarb in spring, just over a year after transplanting. They were surprisingly thick compared to those limp offerings in the supermarket, and the leaves looked like giant fans.

You could leave rhubarb to grow naturally and pick around a third of the stems in April, but for the best results I use a technique called "forcing." Now it's time for a history lesson. In the 1870s, rhubarb farmers in an area of Yorkshire known as the Rhubarb Triangle (between Leeds, Bradford, and Wakefield) figured out a method of improving the taste of harvested stems. This forcing process involved covering up rhubarb plants as they developed in spring. Without access to light, the leaves remained yellow and the nutrients that the plant would have used for leaf growth traveled back down the stems, making them far more vibrant and juicy than those exposed to daylight.

Those Yorkshire rhubarb farmers would build special "dark" sheds for their crop. My little patch doesn't need quite so much coverage. Instead of buying traditional terracotta rhubarb forcers, I reuse what I already have on hand: large, black plastic plant tubs. You could also use a metal garbage can or an upturned box. In late winter, I place a tub over a third of my plants, making sure not to cover the same area as last year because this will stress and weaken them. I leave the tub in place for 4–5 weeks, until mid-March, for an early crop. Once removed, I am left with the most delicious, tender stems, which I pull gently but firmly from the base.

Forced or not, garden-grown rhubarb is vibrant, with stems three times the thickness of those in supermarkets. And the taste? To date, no store-bought stems have ever come close. As they say in Yorkshire, "That'll do."

Opposite, left
Uncovering my forced rhubarb and seeing its bright red stems is one of the highlights of March.

Opposite, right
When you pull the stems, try to ensure a small piece of the white crown still remains attached.

Left Don't take more than a third of the stems from each crown at a time, or you risk weakening the plants.

Kitchen tip

The moral of the rhubarb story is "never say never." From once hating the stuff, my family and I now absolutely love rhubarb cake: tart yet fragrant, with a golden soft crust and chunks of bright pink rhubarb. And it's not just us who enjoy it. I once shared the recipe on Instagram and in a magazine column, and now every year without fail it becomes the talk of the spring season.

SUMMER

Sunny days and warm nights combine to create summer's much-anticipated produce. Alas—if only it were possible to enjoy this colorful harvest all year long!

EGGPLANT

Solanum melongena

Originating in southern India, the eggplant has had a long history of cultivation. Its name in the UK, aubergine, derives from the Catalan *alberginia,* which comes from the Arabic *al-bādinjān*—which in turn has roots in Persian and Sanskrit. This is certainly a well-traveled vegetable!

As a child growing up in a hot country, I really hated eggplants and wished my mother would stop growing these awful-tasting fruiting vegetables. She told me my tastebuds would change and she was right. Now a few years older and maybe a little wiser too, I cannot get enough of them. Back in Zambia, eggplants just grew handsomely without any fuss, and I remember there were orange marigolds on either side of the rows. Little did I know that these flowery bookends were the key to a successful eggplant harvest! Thanks, mom.

Sowing and repotting

It's early January: the formalities of wishing everyone a "Happy New Year" are over and the heat mat is rolled out,

Rekha's favorites

'Black Beauty'
'De Barbentane'
'Rosa Bianca'
'Slim Jim'
'White Casper'

ready for the seed trays. At this time of the year there's not much to do on the plot: the ground is either wet or frozen, the greenhouse is taking care of the winter salad, and I'm getting itchy fingers. Fortunately, eggplants require a long growing season so I have the perfect excuse to start them off now. First, I pop compressed coir pellets in tepid water to soak, mimicking the warm, moist environment the seeds would naturally germinate in. I grow just five plants, one each of five different varieties, and sowing them in individual coir pellets is more economical than in trays of seed-starting mix. While the pellets slowly expand, I open my seed box and—like choosing the biggest, foil-wrapped chocolate—take my time deciding which variety of eggplant to sow first.

After gently squeezing the presoaked pellets to remove excess water, I write up the labels; then, using a small bamboo stick, I create two small holes in the spongy pellet, about ½in (1cm) deep. In go two seeds; the second is an insurance policy in case the first fails to germinate. Even when I've nestled the pellets in a propagator with grow lamps overhead and the heat mat underneath, these babies can really test my patience, and sometimes germination can take up to 30 days! But once this has happened, the seedlings grow very

Above To ripen fully, eggplants need the heat and humidity of a greenhouse. My potted plants stand in a deep tray so that I can water from the base.

Below After a five-minute soak, each coir pellet will be home to two eggplant seeds.

 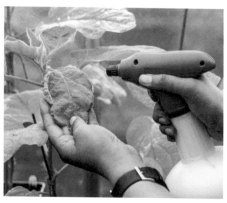

Far left Eggplants are potted when they have two pairs of true leaves.

Left If aphids succeed in attacking the young eggplant leaves, I spray them with soapy water.

quickly in the propagator's warmth, with the first pair of true leaves appearing in just seven days. Two weeks later, when I see a second pair of leaves and roots are emerging from the pellet's fabric casing, I drop the whole pellet into 2¾in (7cm) pots with a little peat-free potting mix in the bottom. Then, with one hand protecting the leaves, I fill the pot and gently firm mix around the plant, taking care to avoid the fragile stem, and water them using a small can, minus the rose attachment so that I don't get the leaves wet. The pots then go back into the propagator.

Growing

By late March, I transfer the growing plants into slightly larger pots—3½in (9cm) is perfect because water is quickly taken up by the roots rather than being washed down to the bottom of a bigger pot. The propagator lid is also removed but the stillness of the indoor air attracts aphids to the plants. My solution is to position an electric oscillating fan about 16in (40cm) from the plants on a slow speed. This not only disturbs the air and the aphids, but helps the stems become sturdy, which would naturally happen outdoors.

In mid-April, two weeks before the plants move to the greenhouse, I feed them with well-diluted liquid seaweed (3–4 drops diluted in 2 pints/1 liter water). This nutrient boost will help them adjust to their new home. Also, the day before the plants' big move, I shade the greenhouse so that the tender leaves aren't scorched by strong sunshine (see p73). Once the eggplants are settled in the greenhouse, they are watered regularly, and any aphids on the leaves are eradicated with a weak solution of soap and water (see above).

By mid-May, when the plants have fully acclimatized, I repot them into 2-gallon (10-liter) pots, label each variety, and arrange them all proudly. By July, I notice my first eggplant flowers emerge, and that's when I need to start a weekly feed of liquid seaweed as well as keep up with watering duties.

Perfect partner: marigolds

I grow pollinator-friendly plants all around the greenhouse so that bees and other insects can get inside the open door. If bees aren't visiting the eggplant flowers, I'll lure them in with a few potted marigolds, close to the plants.

Harvesting

Around the beginning of August, the first eggplants are ready, but I don't leave them on the plants for long and harvest when they are medium-sized and shiny. Eggplants with dull skins indicate the fruit is over-ripe and will taste bitter. My five plants keep producing until late September and I chop any excess fruits into small chunks, then freeze. They'll come in handy for a spicy curry in winter.

Right Eggplants take around seven months to reach maturity, but the smooth, glossy fruits are well worth the wait.

Kitchen tip

I love to grill thick slices of fresh eggplant and serve them with grilled halloumi, salad, and lashings of my special sweet-sour sauce made with soy, ketchup, honey, spices, and pomegranate molasses. Heaven, and not a steak in sight!

CUCUMBER

Cucumis sativus

My very first container-grown cucumber plant had a challenging life. Tucked away in a shady corner of the back garden, it was protected by netting from the children's flying footballs. Even so, it produced a crop of fruit.

Taking on the allotment, I then moved on to smaller pickling cucumbers, which we call gherkins, because I wanted to create brines and make my own pickled gherkins, or pickled anything for that matter. Store-bought pickles have never been my favorite.

Both types are harvested in summer, and when I'm eating freshly picked cucumbers in salads, I'm also thinking about different pickling spices for the gherkins. You can keep your shelves of designer shoes and handbags; what floats my boat are jars of preserved gherkins lined up for winter!

Sowing and hardening off
Both cucumber and gherkin seeds are sown undercover in April (when I sow my zucchini). At this time, the warmth of

the greenhouse kick-starts germination, which happens in just a week. I sow two seeds, pointy end facing down, in a 3½in (9cm) pot; I choose this size over 2¾in (7cm) because the seedlings will grow rapidly and produce their first pair of true leaves within days. Cucumbers also hate root disturbance, so starting them in slightly larger pots reduces the number of times the delicate roots are handled. Then, if both seeds germinate, I remove the weaker one and at the same time insert a 12in (30cm) stick to support the clinging tendrils if these appear early. Within three weeks of germination, the pots have been moved into the cold frame to start their two-week hardening-off period (see p12).

Preparation and planting outside

After sowing, I have a good six weeks to prepare the final growing spot for both crops. This is the same as for zucchini (see p95), including marking out the final planting positions with bamboo canes. I also erect a frame at least 5ft (1.5m) tall, complete with strings for the cucumber plants to climb up, rather than allowing

Above After removing the weaker cucumber seedling, I repot it for the allotment plant sale.

Left To keep the strings taut for the tendrils to climb up, I bury the lower ends beneath the young cucumber plants.

Garden tip

I grow my cucumbers and gherkins outdoors, not in the greenhouse. Outdoor-grown plants (as opposed to indoor-grown) always bear more male than female flowers. Too many male flowers on one plant can produce bitter-tasting fruit, so I snip them off to leave just one for every two female flowers on each plant.

the long stems, with their clinging tendrils, to sprawl along the ground.

Both cucumbers and gherkins have similar growing requirements, but I never plant the two crops together because insects will carry pollen from one to the other. This results in fruits with bitter skins and pulp, so I grow cucumbers and gherkins at different ends of the plot.

In my area, the threat of overnight frost has passed by mid-May, when it's safe to plant cucumbers and gherkins outside. Having watered the plants the day before, they are well hydrated by early morning, which is the best time for planting. After making a 6in- (15cm-) deep hole with my trowel, I gently tap the pot to release the plant, teasing the roots out a little if they are spiralling around. Then I gently lower the plant into its hole next to the structure I created earlier, before backfilling and firming the soil around each plant. Once in place, I give everything a good watering. Soon the tendrils will attach themselves to the string supports and climb upward.

Routine care

To date, my plants haven't suffered slug damage, but as a precaution I'll set a beer trap (see p10) close by. I also make sure the soil around the cucumbers and gherkins is always moist so that the plants remain hydrated. Then, as with most fruiting vegetables, when the first flowers appear, I start the biweekly homemade comfrey feed (see p8), alternating it with liquid seaweed.

Look closely at the flowers and you will see there are two types: male and female. Female flowers have a tiny swelling behind them, which will develop into a fruit when the flower is pollinated. It's a good idea to remove most of the male flowers, leaving just enough on each plant for successful pollination (see Garden tip, p61).

Harvesting

It doesn't take long for the swelling fruits to ripen: my gherkins will be ready to pick in June, and cucumbers a month later, in July. I harvest cucumbers when the fruit is about 4–4¾in (10–12cm) long, whereas gherkins are picked when they are just 2–2½in (5–6cm) in length. At this size, whole gherkins fit perfectly into my jars when I pickle them. The more I pick, the more flowers and fruit are produced—so many that I sometimes miss one. Spotting a runaway gherkin that looks like a small balloon makes a great talking point, but I'll remove it immediately so it doesn't take all the nutrients from the plant.

Right After pollination of the female flowers, fruiting is very speedy. I check for ripe gherkins daily.

Below Pick outdoor cucumbers before they get too large for sweet-tasting flesh, and always remove tough skin.

Kitchen tip

My dear younger sister, Divya, gave me a great tip for using up over-ripe cucumbers. Peel away the hard skin and remove the central watery seed sacs, then grate the remaining pulp and squeeze out any excess water. You can then add the pulp to a batter mix to make fritters or even savory pancakes. What a genius recipe! Thanks, Sis.

TOMATO

Solanum lycopersicum

I'd never grown tomatoes before I got my allotment. When I tasted the freshly picked fruit, I realized what I'd been missing. Forget those force-fed, plumped-up store varieties that have traveled for miles before landing on the shelves; they are tasteless by comparison. I garden organically and grow my tomatoes outdoors. Although the harvest is smaller than if I grew under cover, I know exactly what has gone into producing it. Having trialed so many varieties, I've identified four must-grow tomatoes: one for salads, one to enhance curry sauces, one for strained sauce, and a flavorful, bite-sized cherry. Yet I can't resist sowing another two or three types, just for fun!

Sowing and repotting

Rolling up my sleeves in mid-February, right after Valentine's Day, I start off my tomato seeds in presoaked coir pellets (see p71). After making a hole with a cocktail stick, I drop two seeds into each, cover over with coir, label the pellets, and place them in the propagator with

Rekha's favorites

Determinate (bush)
'Honey Delight'
'Indigo Cherry'

Indeterminate (vining)
'Black Beauty'
'Costoluto Fiorentino'
'Gardeners' Delight'
'Shirley'

Garden tip
. . . .

When tomato seedlings are
first potted, I recommend
burying the stem right up to
the first pair of true leaves. The
hairs on the stem are actually
fine roots, which take up
additional water and nutrients
once they come into contact
with moisture in the soil. The
result is a plant with strong
roots that is well anchored.

Left If you grow
tomatoes outdoors
rather than under
cover, wait until well
after the last frost
before planting
them outside.

Below I recommend
rehydrating coir
pellets with tepid
water to preserve
warmth around
the seedlings.

the heat mat underneath. The seedlings germinate
within just five days, at which point I remove the lid and
position grow lights over them. After another 10 days,
the first pair of true leaves develops. Throughout this
growing stage I make sure the coir pellets don't dry out
by rehydrating them in a saucer of fresh water.

By mid-March (week four), when the second set of true
leaves emerges, I remove the weaker of the two seedlings
and grow it for the allotment plant sale. Then, I transfer
each whole pellet into a 2¾in (7cm) pot of peat-free
potting mix, tap to remove air pockets, and water from
above without wetting the leaves. The seedlings stay on
the mat under the lights until the end of March, when
I transfer them to 2-pint (1-liter) pots so they don't get
rootbound while awaiting planting outdoors.

Understanding tomato types

Determinate (a.k.a. bush) tomatoes are spreading plants
that produce fruit at the end of several side shoots.

Cherry tomatoes fall into this category and some varieties grow well in hanging baskets. Indeterminate (a.k.a. vining) tomatoes, the other principal type, have a single, main stem that grows upright. Some indeterminate varieties do better when grown in a greenhouse or polytunnel, but others are far happier growing outdoors.

Perfect partners: basil and marigold

These two plants not only give off a pungent aroma that keeps tomato pests, such as aphids, at bay, they also aid pollination. Even though basil (see pp98–99) doesn't perform well outdoors here, I still plant it in between the tomato rows. When it flowers, the bees are happy.

Planting outside

If I grew tomatoes in the greenhouse I'd repot them in early May into 2-gallon (10-liter) containers and tuck a basil plant into each pot. But I grow outdoor varieties, so I need to prepare their growing area, which was occupied by brassicas before I cleared the crop in mid-March. After digging over this area, I spread homemade compost on the surface, and leave it to settle. Planting outside must wait until the risk of overnight frost has passed (mid-May in my area), so at the beginning of May I begin the young

Above Also known as tagetes, marigolds are great for pest control in the organic garden.

Below right Fresh comfrey leaves are rich in nitrogen, potassium, and phosphorus—all essential nutrients for healthy growth.

Below far right The tomato plants will soon put on lots of healthy growth, thanks to the decomposing comfrey leaves.

tomato plants' two-week hardening off process (see p12). Then, a week before planting outside, I return to the planting area and break up any large clods of soil before raking the surface level.

On planting-outside day, the first thing I do is head over to the comfrey patch to harvest the leaves that will feed the tomato plants as they grow. Back at the planting area, I dig a hole at least 12in (30cm) deep for each tomato plant and then fill it to the halfway point with comfrey leaves, topping with a thin layer of soil to help the nutritious leaves rot down and feed the tomato plant's roots. In goes the tomato plant, with a taller supporting cane added after firming the soil well with my hands. I allow 20in (50cm) between each plant and on either side of the row I plant their companions, basil and marigold. After a good watering to settle in all the plants, I set a beer trap (see p10) to lure slugs away.

Above Side shoots form at a 45-degree angle to the main growing stem on indeterminate tomatoes. Keep removing them as they grow.

Routine care

Whether indoor- or outdoor-grown, once indeterminate tomatoes get going they will need tying in. I use twine, attaching the stem to the cane just above a leaf node in a figure of eight with the knot resting on the cane. This isn't necessary with the spreading determinate types. I'm also a stickler for order, feeding all my tomatoes on the

Kitchen tip

When everything goes to plan and my tomato harvest is plentiful, I'll make a big batch of a thick, spicy sauce (or ketchup as my sons call it). Cherry tomatoes also freeze well. Put them, whole, into freezer bags and when you are ready to use them, simply defrost and peel away the skin.

same day of the week, every week, once the first flowers appear. I also spoil them a little by alternating between liquid seaweed and comfrey feed. As for watering, I always use a can (to which I add the feed) rather than a hose so that I know how much each plant has received. It's important to water tomato plants regularly because erratic watering can lead to a disease called blossom-end rot, and a spoiled harvest. My tomatoes get a full 2-gallon (10-liter) can weekly, which is enough for three plants.

The final routine task is the removal of side-shoots (see p67), so all the plant's energy goes into producing good-sized fruits on the main stem.

Trusses (clusters) of small flowers soon turn into fruits, and by early August the lower fruits change from dark to light green. On indeterminate varieties, I'll snip off the growing tip once I see 6–7 trusses. This helps all the tomatoes ripen before the days shorten and the weather cools.

Once the first fruits have formed, I also keep my eyes peeled for signs of blight: random scorch marks on leaves that looked fine the previous day and brown patches on fruit. If this disease has taken hold, I uproot affected plants and burn them. Never add diseased plants to the compost heap because the spores will persist in the compost.

Harvesting

Having started off my tomato seeds in February, I can be picking fruit by mid-August. The sight of strong plants with ripe tomatoes hanging down like heavy church bells makes me want to celebrate what I've achieved—with help from Mother Nature, of course!

In early September, while still on the lookout for blight, I cut down on both watering and feeding. And if all my plants stay healthy until the fruit is picked by the end of the month, I love to plan how I'll use my bumper harvest.

Top left My colorful harvest includes 'Indigo Cherry', yellow 'Honey Delight', and tiny 'Texas Wild'.

Center I check plants daily, using sharp snips to pick any red 'Burmese Sour' tomatoes.

Right The specific shade of each tomato variety slowly deepens as the fruit ripens.

Far right Dramatic and exotic when ripe, 'Black Beauty' is a real eye-catcher.

Bottom Given a warm summer, outdoor tomatoes, from bite-sized cherry to beefsteak and plum, should crop abundantly.

CHILE

Capsicum annuum

Spicy food was the norm during my childhood, and when I took on my allotment plot I was determined to make a particular hot sauce that I love, using my own, homegrown chiles. But how to grow them, which varieties to choose, which pot size, and how many to grow of each? Thanks to Rajni, I had a greenhouse, which is the perfect environment in which to grow chiles in my area, but I didn't know how to get the best from it. Panic soon set in.

That first year was a very steep learning curve. No one mentioned ventilation or greenhouse pests, and I made more mistakes than I have fingers to count them on! Gradually, I was able to manage conditions in the greenhouse, including creating shading from hot summer sun (see p73). More importantly, I also learned how to care for the plants inside. Before too long I was rewarded with an abundant chile harvest, the colorful fruit hanging down from the plants like Christmas ornaments. But if you don't have a greenhouse, never fear—you can still grow chiles successfully in pots on a sunny windowsill.

Rekha's favorites

'Chiltepin'
'Kashmiri'
'Scotch Bonnet'
'Tabasco'

Sowing and repotting

I'm always itching to sow chile seeds (as well as eggplant and sweet pepper seeds) right after the Christmas festivities, but I resist—the decorations are still up and I can't deal with too much clutter. But as soon as the tree is put away in January, I roll out the heat mat, wash the propagator trays and lids, and set them aside to dry. With music playing on the radio, I open my box of seeds and select the varieties of chiles I'd like to grow. Like every gardener, I'm always tempted by a few new chile varieties that weren't on my original list, even when there isn't space for them on my annual growing plan. New varieties are such fun to try and might even make it onto my seed list for the following year.

I start off chiles in coir pellets that I presoak in tepid water to swell the compressed disks, then squeeze out excess moisture. After making a small hole in the center of each pellet with a cocktail stick, I drop in a seed, then tuck it into its bed by pulling the coir back over and tapping the top. This helps the seed make good contact with the coir. I always label each pellet immediately so that

Above These long, 'Byadagi' chiles can be picked when young and green or left to mature and turn red.

Below, left Coir pellets soak up a lot of water but need to be just moist, not dripping, or the seeds may rot.

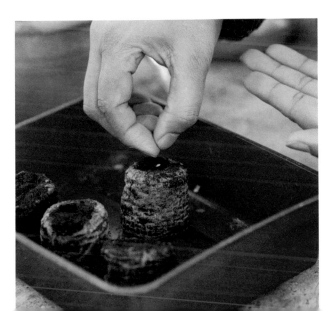

Garden tip

Coir pellets dry out quickly, especially when they are sitting on the heat mat 24/7, so once a week I place each into a small pot of water. As soon as I see that the top of the pellet is moist, I set it aside to drain, then put it back in the covered tray. You can water the pellets using this method both before and after germination. Never be tempted to squeeze them because you might damage the fragile root and shoot.

the varieties don't get mixed up, put them all into the propagator, and then straight onto the heat mat.

Once I notice a tiny green tip peeping out of the pellet, the propagator lid is removed and the overhead grow lights are turned on to create an incubator. The rate of germination will depend on the variety: I find the hotter the chile, the longer this can take—up to 30 days for some seeds. Patience is key.

Outdoor conditions are far from ideal for these heat-loving plants, so my seedlings will enjoy the comfort of their mat and grow lights for the next four months. When the second pair of true leaves appears I repot them, lowering each whole pellet into a 2¾in (7cm) pot, then carefully fill around the sides with seed-starting mix. I always tap the pot to help remove air pockets, gently firm in the mix, then set the pots in a tray and water from the base. Back they go, onto the heat mat under the grow lights, until the end of March when I repot them again. This time the pots are slightly larger at 3½in (9cm), and filled with peat-free, multipurpose potting mix.

Growing

Around the end of April my chile plants are ready to be moved to high school (a.k.a. "the greenhouse"), but first I need to create shading so that the delicate leaves, which have known only artificial light, aren't scorched by strong UV rays. Rather than apply a chemical-based shading paint, my "make-do and mend" choice is the green protective debris netting used around scaffolding in the construction. It's just the right thickness to diffuse the light, and I simply drape it over the whole greenhouse roof, allowing it to fall at least halfway down the sides before securing it in place with small clamps.

During May I spend long days at the allotment, and always leave the greenhouse door wide open. Although it isn't hot outside, the cool breeze flowing into the

Top, left By the time the chile plants move to the greenhouse they have been repotted twice.

Top It's too hot in the greenhouse to repot the chiles for the final time. Pulling up a wheelbarrow of potting mix, I prefer to do this task outside.

Left From late July, I can be harvesting ripe chiles on an almost daily basis.

Above After their long growing season, hanging up ristras of chiles to dry gives me a huge sense of accomplishment.

Kitchen tip

I'm a big fan of making my own chili powder—some years it might be just a tiny 3½oz (100g) jar—and I also like to freeze whole chiles for use in dishes over the winter. But it's the whole, dried pods that give me the most joy: I love to drop them in a stew or use them to temper the oil before making curries the Rekha way.

greenhouse keeps the air moving and helps the plants fight off any lingering pests. I also keep an eye on the moisture content in the pots and water regularly, never letting the potting mix get too dry.

By early May, with my big 2-gallon (10-liter) pots waiting, the chile plants are ready to be repotted into them for the final time. I don't fill the pots to the brim, leaving a gap of 2in (5cm) for watering, which prevents potting mix from spilling out and being wasted. When I arrange the pots on the greenhouse shelves and see all my chile plants settled in their final home, I can't keep from smiling. By July, the plants begin to flower and I start the feeding regimen, always on the same day of the week so I don't forget. My weekly feed alternates between homemade comfrey tea (see p8) and diluted liquid seaweed.

Harvesting

My seeds got a head start on the heat mat in January, so by the end of July, the plants have begun to produce green fruit. After another month these will have started turning red, ready for harvesting.

The key to a long chile harvest is to pick the ripe fruits often, which triggers the production of further flowers and fruits. My harvesting window can last from the end of July right until late October, and the plants provide me with an abundance of chiles. I use them fresh as needed, and thread others on a string, called a ristra, that I hang up in the kitchen or potting shed to dry. I know the chiles on the ristra are thoroughly dry and ready to store in airtight jars when I give each of them a gentle shake and they sound just like a baby's rattle. But before storing, there's one final task. I split some of the pods for next year's sowing. Turning first to my favorites, such as kashmiri and scotch bonnet, I take just two or three seeds from each dried pod. There are plenty left because every pod carries 10 or more fiery seeds.

Right Attractive in both color and shape, ripe chiles have a range of heat levels, from mild to extremely hot.

Bottom Always store whole, dried chiles of the same type together. Also, for a less fiery chili powder, don't add too many seeds.

SWEET PEPPER

Capsicum annuum

To bring out their crisp, juicy sweetness, sweet bell peppers need a long growing season, which they certainly don't get when grown speedily for the supermarkets. I start sowing at the beginning of the year, and although the fruits won't be ripe until July, their superb flavor, color, and texture make them well worth the wait. At first I grew the usual red and green bell peppers, but dropped them with a big thud once I'd sown and harvested the long, pointed types, such as 'Corno di Toro'. They produced far more fruit per plant than regular bell types, and my harvests were so bountiful I had enough to freeze and use over the winter. In the past couple of years, new bell varieties have caught my eye and I've had success with 'Cardinal', an intense purple, almost black, pepper.

Rekha's favorites

Bell
'Cardinal'
'Sweet Chocolate'
Pointed
'Corno di Toro Giallo'
'Nardello'

Sowing and repotting

Pepper seeds germinate quickly, within two weeks. That means there's no real rush to sow them, but I just can't wait, and during January and February the dining table

becomes my workstation. At one end are coir pellets ready to be soaked in a dish of tepid water, at the other the propagator trays are waiting, and in the middle are my seed packets, plant labels, and marker pen. As with chiles (see p71), after presoaking the pellets, I make a hole, insert the seed, and then label. The propagator tray then goes on the heat mat where the pepper seeds will join trays of eggplant and chile seeds, also sitting snugly inside their pellets. I'm so excited to have started off the gardening year that I can't resist peeping inside the propagators later that same day, just to see if any seeds have already germinated!

After germination—once the green stem of each seedling sits above the soil as the true leaves stretch out—I take off the lid and return the tray back to the heat mat, under the grow lamps. The light will help trigger photosynthesis and encourage strong, short stems. Within a week the first pair of true leaves appears, and seedlings are transferred into 2¾in (7cm) pots of peat-free potting mix. For stability, I bury the seedling up to the base of these leaves, then tap the base of the pot to remove air pockets before watering the seedlings, and put the pots back under the lamps.

Routine care
From the day they germinate in January until the end of April, the peppers will remain in the house, but I try to replicate the outdoor environment by passing my hand

Left A tray of warm water is ideal for presoaking and expanding dry coir pellets, ready for sowing.

Below Pepper seedlings look very similar, so label each variety as soon as you've sown it.

Garden tip

During March, before watering your peppers, poke your little finger down the side of the pot and only water if the soil still feels dry more than halfway down. Over-watering will deprive the roots of oxygen and weaken the plant. A good way of checking is to gently remove the plant from its pot and inspect the roots. If they look brown, you need to cut back on the watering.

over the seedlings several times a day. This moves the air around them, like a gentle breeze, also disturbs any whitefly or aphids, and it's a good excuse to get close to my plants.

Once a third set of true leaves starts to appear, I give my pepper seedlings a very weak feed of organic liquid seaweed (3–4 drops diluted in 2 pints/1 liter of water). Young seedlings can't handle full-strength feed and this gives them the gentle boost they need to grow well and with some vigor. Then, during March, I transfer the young peppers into slightly larger 3½in (9cm) pots to grow until it's time for their final move to the greenhouse in mid-April. If you don't have a greenhouse, a sheltered, sunny spot in the garden will work, or continue growing peppers indoors, moving the pots outside during warm weather and bringing them back indoors at night.

Growing

The young pepper plants soon acclimatize, enjoying the hot, humid environment of the greenhouse, and respond by putting on substantial growth. By mid-May, the plants are ready to be transferred to 2-gallon (10-liter) terracotta pots filled to within 2in (5cm) of the top to allow for watering. I repot the peppers outside (I do the same with eggplants); it's far too hot to work in the greenhouse.

At the onset of flowers 3–4 weeks later, around mid-June, I'll start a weekly feeding regimen. At this stage, the plants need a lot of energy so that they can produce the fruit that follows flowering and successful pollination. This weekly feed (comfrey tea one week, liquid seaweed the next) provides a balance of nutrients and will ensure good fruit formation.

Harvesting

I'm always tempted to harvest the peppers when they are green and glistening, but steel myself to wait until they turn red, purple, yellow, or orange (depending on the variety). I check for ripe fruit at regular intervals and harvest them often, snipping off the stalk close to the plant's stem. Picking encourages more flowers, followed by more fruit. The advantage of starting the seed off in January is a long harvest, and I can enjoy picking from July right through October.

Opposite, far left Water peppers from the base, when they need it, to increase humidity levels around the plants.

Center The open greenhouse door allows pollinators in and fruit soon follows the flowers.

Left Harvest peppers as soon as they are red to speed up ripening of the remaining fruits.

Below Peppers and chiles (see pp70–75) belong to the same family. They grow together in the greenhouse and ripen at similar times.

GREEN BEAN

Phaseolus vulgaris

In summer, the bamboo or hazel poles for my climbing green beans add fantastic structure to the plot. French beans are a type of green bean, and I grow two varieties of them: cylindrical and, my favorite, flat-podded. The twining stems soon scramble up these 6½ft (2m) supports and even creep over to any other neighboring structures.

Yet it wasn't the thought of eating fresh pods that first tempted me. After noticing beautiful, brightly colored dried beans in the supermarket, I just had to find out which plants produced them. Most came from the long pods of the familiar French climbing beans, left on the plant so that the seeds inside developed fully. I couldn't wait to grow them, planning to pick pods to eat fresh and let others mature and store them over winter. Those dried beans were calling me!

Rekha's favorites

'Cyprus'
'Helda' (flat-podded)
'Kew Blue'

Sowing and hardening off

French beans can be sown outdoors around mid-May, but I've found they take forever if I wait until then.

Instead, I get ahead by sowing them in the greenhouse in mid-April, in deep Rootrainers. These cleverly designed containers allow the plants to produce deeper, stonger, more fibrous roots.

Beans are large seeds and I sow them at least twice their depth, water them until the excess runs out of the bottom, then set the Rootrainers on the staging in the greenhouse. The seeds germinate quickly in the warmth, and within a week I notice each seedling has a perfectly formed pair of true leaves.

After two weeks, I transfer the fast-growing plants into the cold frame for their hardening-off period (see p12). Even at this early stage, the plants are showing their vinelike nature by twining around each other. The sooner I can get them into their planting positions, the better!

Planting outside

On the same day I sow the beans in the greenhouse, I prepare their growing area outdoors by digging a square hole 20in (50cm) wide and 12in (30cm) deep. To this I add a 6-8in- (15–20cm-) thick layer of either well-rotted manure or compost to provide nutrients, followed by a scoopful of chicken manure, before I backfill. Once I've raked the surface level, I put up a circular structure using six hazel poles, or eight bamboo canes, each about 8ft (2.5m) in height, and arranged about 8in (20cm) apart. These are pushed down at least 20in (50cm) into the soil for stability, then I secure the tops with twine. The vertical structure starts to give my plot some definition.

Above When the beans inside have dried out fully, the pods open naturally.

Below I bought my first set of Rootrainers six years ago, and it's one of the best investments in gardening equipment I've ever made.

When mid-May arrives, the young beans are ready for planting outside. Trowel in hand, I make a hole on the inside of each cane; this way I won't damage the growing beans with my hoe while weeding. Then, opening the sleeve of the Rootrainer, I carefully lower each plant into its hole, firm the soil around it, and water it. Once all the plants are in place, I open a bottle of warm beer and pour it into a nearby slug trap (see p10). Chin chin!

Routine care

Beans are very thirsty plants, so I never allow the soil around them to dry out. They appreciate a generous watering of at least 2 gallons (10 liters) per climbing structure every third day, and in very hot summers I give them an additional 1–2 gallons (5–8 liters) each evening.

Purple or white flowers, depending on the variety, start to appear from the base of the plants around the end of June. I'm as excited as the bees to see them, and dash into the shed to mix up a liquid seaweed feed. Always apply the feed to damp soil and do it only once a week. Your plants will repay you with plenty of high-quality pods.

Harvesting and storing

I snip off the first pods in late June, always starting from the base where the first flowers appeared. Cylindrical varieties are harvested when the pods are no more than 4–4¾in (10–12cm) in length. Flat-podded varieties are picked when around 6–8in (15–20cm) long, while they are still tender and before I can feel any beans forming within. Both types are very productive, so pick them regularly, before they get too large and the skins become tough.

Although I could carry on harvesting until August, I stop when I've picked pods from all the plants up to a level halfway up the structure. If we can't eat all the freshly picked pods, I'll pickle or freeze the surplus. All pods above the halfway mark are then left on the plant to ripen so that the beans inside mature. I harvest these only when the pods have dried out on the stems, usually in early September before heavy morning dews start to fall. The pods are then laid out in the potting greenhouse to dry out completely, and when they pop open, it's time to collect the beans inside.

Before I store the dry beans, I inspect them for small, translucent patches—these are the telltale signs of bean-weevil attack. If any are spotted (and you could do this as a precaution), I lay the whole batch on a baking tray and chill in the fridge for five to seven days to kill any lurking weevil eggs. The beans are then stored in sterile clip-top jars in a cool, dark cupboard. Another year's harvest has been successfully saved, ready to add to warming, slow-cooked casseroles over winter.

Kitchen tip

Young pods harvested in early summer are best enjoyed lightly steamed and tossed in a summer salad, like tabbouleh. But when we have a Sunday dinner, these pods will be lightly steamed and added to hot mustard oil in a griddle pan, along with a generous sprinkle of hot paprika and garlic salt. Hold the black pepper—you won't need it.

Bottom left Beans have started swelling inside the pods, which will stay on the plant to mature.

Center I can rely on my favorite flat-podded beans for high yields of juicy pods.

Below A fine, dry day is best for harvesting these mature 'Kew Blue' French beans.

ONION

Allium cepa

"Oh, onions are so are easy to grow from sets," veteran plot-holders told me when I first took on my allotment. My plot neighbor a short distance away had fantastic harvests from sets (commercially grown, virus-free baby onions), but they didn't work for me. After three years with nothing to show but failed harvests, I changed tack. Now I've found I can successfully grow both red and white onions, as well as shallots, from seed. Yes, I made mistakes, but over time I perfected the process. Here's how I did it.

First sowing

I sow my onion seeds twice a year: the first batch in February, for a September crop; the second (see p86), done in late summer, overwinters and is ready for harvesting the following summer.

For this first "spring" sowing, I sow seeds indoors in trays or modules filled with fresh seed-starting mix, then cover with a further ½in (1cm) of sieved mix. Onion seeds are small and easily displaced, so I always water from the base

Rekha's favorites

First sowing
'Ailsa Craig'
'Bedfordshire Champion'

Second sowing
'Senshyu'
'Toughball'

(see p98), let the trays drain, then set them in a warm, bright location; a kitchen windowsill is ideal.

Germination takes 6–10 days (sooner if I use my trusty heat mat. Now comes the crucial step: at the very first sign of germination, the tray is swiftly moved into the unheated greenhouse, which is warm in the day but cool at night. This nightly drop in temperature benefits the seedlings and helps produce firm stems. By mid-March, the seedlings are ready to be repotted into 2¾in (7cm) pots, which I move into the cold frame to start the two-week hardening-off process (see p12). While they're in there, I prepare the onions' growing patch by weeding, lightly digging to incorporate air into the soil, and generally creating a fine tilth. .

Planting outside

In early April, on planting-outside day, I start by scattering and then raking some organic bone and blood meal fertilizer into the growing area, applying about 2½oz (70g) per square yard (square meter). I prefer small to medium-sized onions, so I space them quite closely at 8–6in (10–15cm) apart, and allow 16in (40cm) between each row. I then water the seedlings and keep them well

Above Onion seeds will germinate indoors on a bright windowsill.

Below Planted fairly closely, white onions won't grow too large.

Garden tip

I recommend working blood and bone meal into the soil before planting onion seeds outside. After exhausting the food in their pots, the plants are ready to take up nutrients from this slow-release fertilizer.

watered as they establish, but after that I water no more than once a week—and even then only if the soil feels dry. I've found that this "controlled stress" gives the onions a spicy taste. When I watered the crop more regularly, the flavor was milder.

Growing and harvesting

Onions hate competition. Throughout early summer, weeding between and around the plants is vital in order to keep them growing strongly. In mid-June I give the young plants their second and final feed, watering it well. Soon, the bulbs' white stems start to swell at the base—an impressive sight that never fails to put a smile on my face. I know tears will flow later when I cook with my onion harvest. But they'll be happy tears!

Toward the end of July, I stop watering completely. In August, the onions' green tops collapse, telling me it's time to harvest them (I told you my plants talk to me!). Because I've let the area dry out, the plants only need to be gently teased from the soil using a garden fork. Then, after a quick brush to remove excess soil, I place the whole bulbs—stalk and all—upside-down in rows on a tall rack with open wire shelves for good ventilation. This process ensures no moisture collects around the necks, which would cause rot. In September, I like to string my onions and hang them up in the potting shed, where they'll be stored and used from late fall to early spring.

Second sowing

Just as the first harvest is lifted, I sow the winter varieties of onion seed. The process is the same but the seed trays stand outside on my potting bench, where the summer air helps kick-start germination. Given the heat, I keep a close eye on the trays, making sure they don't dry out. By late September, as daytime temperatures start to cool, the seedlings will be repotted and ready to move into the greenhouse. I then leave the seedlings in their 2¾in (7cm) pots to overwinter, keeping watering to a minimum because they won't grow much at all until the following March.

In spring, these overwintered seedlings are ready to be planted outside. While the process is the same, overwintered onions tend to grow faster at this stage than their spring-sown cousins. By early July, their stems collapse, and a week or two later, the harvest can begin.

Perfect partner: lettuce

Intersown between rows of onions, quick-growing lettuce (see pp20–23) can be harvested within weeks, leaving space for the onions to grow well. Meanwhile, the onions' pungent aroma deters aphids from feasting on the lettuce leaves.

Right and below 'Ailsa Craig' is a tried-and-true variety of white onion that can be sown in either spring or fall.

Bottom When the onions on these racks are completely dry, I'll string and hang them up in the traditional way.

SWEET CORN

Zea mays

Throughout my childhood in Zambia, sweet corn (or maize, as it was known there) was my favorite vegetable. I loved it so much that during harvest season, which ran from late November through January, I'd even offer to walk to the vegetable market to pick it up. Having watched my mom choose the best cobs on sale, I knew exactly what to look for, and also how to negotiate the best price. I also learned how to make her fantastic corn chowder—a spicy, thick, gloopy soup. We ate it with crunchy sev, a vermicelli-like savory snack made with chickpea flour.

When I taste my homegrown corn, all those pleasing childhood memories come flooding straight back. As they say, moms are the best!

Rekha's favorites

'Double Red'
'Special Swiss'
'True Gold'

Sowing

April is the month to sow wrinkly, tooth-shaped sweet corn seeds. These are kernels that have been fully dried on the cob, and are best soaked the night before sowing. Soaking has two advantages. First, it's a way of identifying seeds that won't germinate successfully. Those will simply fail to

swell and can be discarded. Second, it stops visiting mice from eating what you've sown. The pests love to snack on dry seeds, rummaging in the greenhouse pots and trays to find them, but for some reason they turn up their noses at seeds that have been soaked.

I use deep Rootrainers filled with gently firmed, peat-free potting mix and sow a single soaked seed about ¾–1¼in (2–3cm) deep in each cell. The seeds are large and won't be dislodged when I water from above. With April daytime temperatures in my greenhouse hitting 68°F (20°C), the seeds take less than a week to germinate and even put on an inch or so of growth. At this point, I move the seedlings into the cold frame for their two-week hardening-off period (see p12), after which they will have developed into tall, sturdy plants, ready to go outdoors.

Planting outside

Back in March, while preparing the plot for other crops, I marked out the sweet corn's eventual planting area and worked in a bucketful each of straw and well-rotted manure. Over the next month, the soil will settle and any weed seeds that decide to germinate will be shown the back (and front) of my hoe! Then, on the day of planting in mid-May, I rake the planting area to break up any remaining clods and add a handful of slow-release blood and bone meal fertilizer. For successful pollination and cob development, it's always best to plant sweet corn in a

Above At the very top of the sweet corn plants, the male tassels are as tall as the sunflowers.

Below Sweet corn germinates very quickly in the warmth of a greenhouse, or on a sunny windowsill.

Kitchen tip

My mother's corn chowder was my childhood comfort food. To taste it again, I grate freshly harvested corn to release the pulp, mix in some spiced oil, followed by fresh ginger and chili, cumin, and salt. After stirring in plain yogurt to thicken, I add a handful of chopped, fresh cilantro. Instant nostalgia!

block or grid formation, rather than in single rows. Wind (not insects) transfers pollen from the male flower (called the tassel) at the top to the silks on the female flowers lower down. Grouping the plants together ensures they catch the wind and all the silks turn into butter-yellow kernels.

I plant the young sweet corn 6in (15cm) deep to anchor the plants as they grow taller and become heavy with cobs. Although seed packets recommend 18in (45cm) intervals for planting, I like to space them closer together, at 14in (35cm). This means I can squeeze in an extra plant without compromising the quality of the harvest.

Routine care

It's important that the soil around the young sweet corn plants remain moist at all times, so I water them regularly, especially in hot weather. Allowing the plants to dry out can trigger premature flowering, which results in short, stumpy plants and, consequently, a poor harvest.

By early August as the cobs start to fatten and mature, I notice birds and squirrels are on the lookout, and they seem to know exactly when the corn is ripe enough to nibble. To keep these predators out and protect my crop, I stretch netting around and over the plants. The netting is supported by bamboo canes pushed into the earth, and the canes are topped with recycled bottles so that the net doesn't snag on them. I then peg the netting down firmly all the way around the base, making sure there are no gaps.

Harvesting

Around mid-August, when I see the soft, cream-colored silks have turned brown and become coarse, I know the corn inside will be ripe and juicy. I take a firm hold of each ripe cob and snap it from the stem. The next task is to get the cobs back to my kitchen as soon as possible. The taste of just-picked corn on the cob is sweeter and fresher than anything you can buy in a supermarket.

Top left With good root systems already established, the sweet corn is planted in a grid formation.

Center Leave space between plants so that you can hoe and keep on top of weeds.

Right Ripe cobs are easy to twist off by hand; there's no need to use pruners.

Bottom As indicated by the brown silks, the creamy kernels are ready to eat.

ZUCCHINI

Curcurbita pepo

If I had to choose one vegetable that made me realize nothing beats the taste of homegrown, it would be the zucchini. Before gardening became a passion, I'd bring home supermarket zucchini, thinking in all honesty that this tasteless vegetable's sole purpose was to add bulk to a dish! If anyone asked me what I thought of them, I'd shrug my shoulders and say: "Well, they're OK." Now, having grown zucchini for 10 years, I really appreciate their unique texture and flavor. In summer, while weeding around the plants' prickly leaves, I've even picked a very young zucchini and munched it like a cucumber. Well, they are from the same family!

Rekha's favorites

'Black Forest'
'Firenze'
'Shooting Star'
'Zephyr'

Sowing

This is one vegetable that does not make it onto my marathon March sowing list. On account of their fast germination rate (within seven days), emerging zucchini seedlings always catch up with other vegetables I started off a month or so earlier.

In April, I fill three 3½in (9cm) pots with peat-free potting mix and sow two seeds per pot at a depth of 1in (2.5cm). I find that two or three zucchini plants, each one a different variety, is plenty for our family. I start them off in the greenhouse (a sunny windowsill indoors also works well). Once the seeds germinate and have two true leaves (about 14 days from sowing), I remove the weakest of the two seedlings, pot these, and set them aside for the allotment plant sale. I then move the pots with stronger seedlings into the cold frame to start the hardening-off process (see p12), and they will stay there until all threat of frost has passed. For my area, that is around mid-May. By the end of this six-week period, the young plants will have grown to a healthy 8in (20cm), the ground will be warmer, and it's time for planting outside.

Preparation and planting outside

Zucchini is a really hungry, thirsty, plant, so when I'm getting the plot ready in March, I always give the intended planting area some extra TLC. After digging over the soil, I create deep planting holes of at least a spade's depth (12in/30cm) for each zucchini. I then add well-rotted compost, plus a handful of chicken manure to each, backfill, and mark the prepared area with a bamboo

Top This zucchini seedling has just one true leaf; the other two are seed leaves.

Bottom Take the rose off when you water zucchini to avoid splashing the leaves and risking fungal disease.

Garden tip

After firming in the young zucchini plants, I like to create a shallow circular channel roughly 8in (20cm) from the stem. This directs the flow from the watering can straight to the plant's roots, so the moisture is not lost to the surrounding soil. Watering a little way from the plant also avoids excess wetting of the stem, which can lead to rotting.

cane. Come May, when I'm ready to plant the zucchini outside, I'll be very glad I marked the exact spot!

On the day before planting, I make sure the zucchini plants are well watered, ready for the move from pot to plot. Next morning, after making a 6in-(15cm-) deep hole with my trowel, I tap the plant out of its pot into my hand, carefully lower it into the hole, backfill, and firm the soil around the stem. After watering (see Garden tip), I lay some straw around the plant to reduce moisture evaporation over the summer months. Finally, I set beer traps (see p10) so that Mr. and Mrs. Slug will enjoy a party and hopefully leave my young, tender plants alone. Fortunately, the slugs will have lost interest by July when the zucchini leaves will have grown larger and coarser, with tiny prickly hairs that irritate their soft underbellies.

Routine care

If I've learned one thing about caring for zucchini, it's never to let the soil around the plants either dry out or become waterlogged. Fluctuating moisture levels will stress the plant and can cause powdery mildew, a fungal disease that appears as a layer of white dust on the upper surface of the leaves. Although it isn't fatal, this disease can limit the leaves' ability to convert sunshine to energy, which results in poor growth, fewer flowers, and smaller fruits. My strategies

for warding off powdery mildew range from performing a "sun dance" in summer to crossing my fingers and thumbs so we don't get sudden downpours of rain!

It doesn't take plants long to establish in the nutrient-rich soil, and within four weeks from planting outside the first flowers start to appear. A frenzy of bee activity around the zucchini plants is a sure sign the flowers are being pollinated and it's time for the plants' first liquid seaweed feed. But before any feed is applied, I always check to make sure the soil is moist. As my mom always says, "Never take medication on an empty stomach," and this advice is also true for my plants, which take up feed more efficiently if they are already hydrated.

Harvesting

By mid-June the zucchini plants have put on a huge amount of growth and the female flowers (the males have a single, pointed stamen in the center) start to swell at the base and form fruits.

Zucchini is ready to harvest when the fruits are 4–6in (10–15cm) long, or slightly larger than a tennis ball for the round varieties. Keep picking and the plants will produce further flowers and fruits right up until the end of August—which can be a problem if you planted too many. Having grown just three zucchini plants, I'm one of the few people on the allotment who isn't complaining of a glut!

Top right Following pollination, the area behind the female flowers swells and fruits start to form.

Far right 'Shooting Star' is a yellow zucchini with tasty flesh and an upright growing habit.

Bottom Zucchini is so productive that just three plants will keep the family well supplied all through summer.

Kitchen tip

My zucchini and chocolate cake—moist, gooey, and delicious—is always popular in our house. But before I even think of baking, I turn my attention to those delightful yet delicate butter-yellow flowers. Picking a couple of male flowers—these have pollen-rich stamens in the center, which I snip off—I add them whole to an omelette before folding it over so they steam lightly for a minute. Garnish with fresh cut-and-come-again lettuce leaves for a simple, delicious lunch.

BASIL

Ocimum basilicum

Basil is an herb I just cannot do without. In the summer months I behave like a locust, stripping the plants of leaves either to use fresh, or for drying and using over the winter. When I was introduced to Thai cuisine, the distinct fragrance of Thai basil blew me away, and I also love the fiery punch of Greek basil. These two, along with sweet basil, are my go-to varieties.

Sowing and potting on

Included in my big March sowing is a tray with three perfectly labeled rows of basil seeds—one each of sweet, Greek, and Thai varieties. Basil seeds are tiny, so I put a label where each row starts. Then, taking a very small pinch of seeds, I sow each variety using the label as the starting point. After covering lightly with sieved seed-starting mix, I place the seed tray in a bigger tray full of water so that the mix is saturated from the base. This ensures none of the tiny seeds are displaced. After removing the tray and letting excess water drain away, I put it in the greenhouse. A warm, bright windowsill would also work well.

Within 10 days the basil seeds have germinated. As the weather warms, I continue watering from the base to ensure that the mix doesn't dry out. Once the seedlings

Garden tip

The strong scent of basil deters pests, so I grow them as near to my eggplants as possible to ward off greenhouse whitefly and aphids. I also plant basil among my outdoor tomatoes (see pp64–69) for the same reason.

Rekha's favorites

Sweet
Greek
'Horapha Nanum' (Thai)

have two sets of true leaves, I transfer them into individual 2¾in (7cm) pots of peat-free potting mix, water them, and put the pots back on the greenhouse staging.

Growing

My plants thrive in the humid greenhouse, where they also appreciate the shade I've provided from the hot sun (see p73). Around six weeks later, in mid-May, I repot the basil plants again, this time into 3½in (9cm) pots, pinching out the tops to encourage side shoots for a bushier plant. At this point, they get a weak feed of nettle tea for healthy leaf growth. By June, the plants are sturdy and repotted for the last time into 8-pint (5-liter) pots.

Harvesting

The joy of growing basil is that it can be harvested as soon as the plants are 4in (10cm) high, but I wait until they are more established and have reached 10–12in (25–30cm). By taking leaves from the top to promote the growth of new side shoots farther down the stem, I manage to extend the harvest through October.

Top left The young basil plants are transferred into terracotta pots, which are more porous than plastic.

Above 'Mammoth' is a variety of basil with huge, very aromatic, crinkled leaves.

Bottom This small selection includes Greek basil (second from left) and sweet basil (far right).

Kitchen tip

My all-time favorite way of using fresh basil is in the Italian *insalata caprese*. After pounding the leaves with a little rock salt and then adding extra-virgin olive oil, I drizzle the vibrant green sauce over sliced beefsteak tomatoes and mozzarella. This dish simply shouts "summer is here!"

GARLIC

Allium sativum

I remember planting my very first garlic crop as if it were yesterday. It was summer, I got the keys to a half-plot on the allotment, and the whole family (my irritable teenagers included) were helping clear bindweed and couch grass from my small but overgrown piece of heaven. The work was backbreaking and there were some tearful moments, yet by September, when the ground was ready, I was determined to start growing. But what could I sow over fall and winter with the main growing season over? I was still quite new to gardening then, and (to be honest) only a fair-weather gardener, but after consulting my trusted old gardening books, I found it was the perfect time to plant garlic. So, I bought a few different garlic seed bulbs, broke them into cloves, and then planted them in the newly cleared ground of my plot.

Understanding garlic types

Supermarkets don't use "hardneck" or "softneck" to describe their garlic, and when I started gardening I had

Rekha's favorites

Hardneck
'Carcassonne'
'Rose Wight'

Softneck
'Germidour'
'Solent Wight'

no idea what these terms meant. Put simply, the "neck" is the stem. Hardneck garlic has strong, erect stems that become stiff when dried. It produces large, strong-tasting, pungent bulbs that dry well but are best used by mid-winter. Softneck types have soft stems that are flexible enough to be braided when dried. Although the softneck bulbs are smaller and with a milder taste than hardneck varieties, they store well through winter and into spring. I grow both types.

Sowing and planting outside

The usual advice is to plant individual garlic cloves of both types directly in the ground (pointed end uppermost). This method proved successful on my first half-plot, but after moving a short distance to a new, full-sized plot, my garlic crop struggled. Poor drainage on this plot, together with wetter winters from that year onward, meant the soil remained sodden and my garlic began to rot. I had to give up on direct sowing after that.

Instead, each September, I plant individual cloves at twice their depth in 3½in (9cm) pots of potting mix, and keep them under cover until the following spring. Garlic needs a cold spell to germinate, and although my pots are in the greenhouse, the temperature is cold enough over winter for germination to take place. If your plot or garden has good drainage and the soil is not too heavy, direct sowing in either September or October, at the same depth as indoor-sown cloves, should be fine.

In March, I prep the area where the garlic will grow by digging its covering of overwintering green manure (see p8) back into the soil to rot down and add nutrients. By the end of April, I'm ready to plant my garlic seedlings at intervals of 4in (10cm), using a stringline for a straight row. I allow 12in (30cm) spacing between each row for good air circulation, and make sure the two different types of garlic are separated. After watering, the plants will establish and put on growth over the spring months.

Top Once you've harvested your first garlic crop, set aside a bulb so you can plant your own cloves in the fall.

Bottom I don't recommend planting cloves from supermarket garlic. It isn't guaranteed disease-free and may have been chemically treated.

Garden tip

In addition to watering sparingly and never from above, allowing plenty of space between garlic plants will also help prevent rust. Also, I strongly recommend that you not grow garlic in the same place every year to avoid the buildup of fungal spores in the soil (see p10).

Left Space out garlic plants so you can get a hoe between them for regular weeding.

Bottom By July, the garlic's top growth has started to yellow and die—a sure sign the bulbs beneath won't grow any further.

Opposite top and center Always use a fork to uproot garlic so you don't damage the stems, and never wash off soil. The bulbs must be kept dry for storage.

Opposite right Don't trim the stems of softneck garlic after harvesting. When dry, they are pliable enough to create a traditional plait or braid.

Routine care

When the weather warms, I keep watering to a minimum and avoid splashing the garlic leaves by removing the rose from the can. Directing the flow around the base of the plant helps prevent the fungal disease known as rust. Its spores are present in the soil, so watering garlic from above risks droplets bouncing back up from the ground and transferring rust spores to the undersides of the leaves. I also keep the planting area free of weeds, especially in June when it's time to feed the plants (but not the weeds) with a scattering of slow-release blood and bone meal fertilizer, in the quantities recommended on the package, around the stems.

Allium leaf-miner flies (see p176) are on the wing from March to April and again from September to November, but by planting garlic in late April and harvesting before September, I avoid having to cover the plants with netting to keep the flies off.

Harvesting

When garlic leaves turn yellow and look lifeless, it's time to stop watering altogether and allow the plants to die back, ready for harvesting. The softneck varieties will even collapse, as though they've given up on life! Choosing a dry afternoon, I carefully dig up the bulbs with a garden fork, shake off the soil, and lay them out in the potting shed, where it's dry and bright but out of direct sunlight. After leaving them to dry for a week or two, I prepare to store the bulbs, starting with the hardneck varieties. I brush off any remaining soil and cut away some of the dried roots, as well as remove most of the stem, leaving about 8in (10cm) still attached to the bulbs. These I tie in small bundles and hang up in the cool garage. With the softneck varieties, I trim the roots, grade them by bulb size, and then braid the stems. I recommend starting with the largest bulb and working down to the smallest, using roughly 12 bulbs per braid.

Kitchen tip

My daughter's favorite dish is spicy garlic shrimp, flash-fried in hot oil with turmeric, chili, mango powder, and plenty of crushed, homegrown garlic. Finish with a squeeze of lemon, garnish with lots of roughly chopped cilantro (or not, in my daughter's case!), and dig in. I promise they'll be the best shrimp you've ever tasted!

GARDEN PEA

Pisum sativum

Rekha's favorites

'Alderman'
'Douce Provence'
'Hurst Greenshaft'
'Meteor' (dwarf variety)

Easy to grow and not requiring tall supports (especially the dwarf varieties), peas are a great option for first-time vegetable growers. They are at their absolute sweetest when freshly picked and cooked for the minimum of time, but getting them from your plot to the kitchen can be difficult. This is why gardeners say peas are the hardest vegetables to "save."

I agree. Every time I harvest the ripe pods, I'm tempted to slide the fresh green peas straight into my mouth. Resistance in my case is futile: the only solution would be to tape my mouth shut before I go near my pea plants! Yet I rarely feel guilty munching my peas in the allotment, because my family doesn't like them at all. I know. How can you not like fresh peas? Oh well, more for me!

Sowing undercover

By early March, I've sanitized the greenhouse and given it a thorough spring cleaning. Now it's time to sow peas, which don't mind cold temperatures. After filling Rootrainers with peat-free potting mix, I sow a single pea in each, at a depth of 1½–2in (4–5cm).

Germination takes less than two weeks, and as soon as this happens, I move the seedlings in their Rootrainers out of the greenhouse into the cold frame, and start the hardening-off process (see p12). As the young peas acclimatize to outdoor temperatures, they continue to put on healthy green growth.

Planting outside

In early April, on the day of planting outside, I add a bucket of garden compost to the area where the peas will grow and work it into the soil. I then mark out a row with my stringline and plant the seedlings along one side of the string at 4in (10cm) intervals. After firming in each plantin the row, I remove the string and start another row, 6–8in (15–20cm) away from the first. Because these rows are fairly close to each other, the twining pea tendrils will latch onto each other and provide support as they grow. Even so, at this point I also give them a little help by inserting a few spent raspberry canes among the seedlings. After watering, I put down a beer trap (see p10) close to the tender seedlings.

Garden tip

Peas are a cool-season crop. They can be sown undercover as early as February, but I prefer to wait and sow a month later in early March. By the time my peas are hardened off and ready to plant outside, the soil won't be so wet and the plants will get off to a good start.

Below, left When filling deep Rootrainers, my potting bench catches any excess potting mix; none is wasted.

Below I've found peas germinate successfully in the greenhouse, so there's no need to sow two per cell.

Right In August, I create a wide trench with my draw hoe for the outdoor-sown peas.

Far right Seed peas are sown in a double row so that they will support each other as they grow taller.

Garden tip

In May, the pea moth wakes from hibernation and the females are active from early to late summer, laying their eggs on pea plants that are in flower. The resulting maggots burrow into the tender pods and eat the developing peas. My early and late-sown crops, which flower outside the moth's egg-laying period, won't be damaged.

Opposite right Peas are best eaten when absolutely fresh, which means as soon as I open the pod!

Far right Tiny peas are forming in the pods, but it will be another 3–5 weeks before they are ripe.

Bottom Spent raspberry canes add extra support when the plants are heavy with ripe peapods.

Direct sowing and routine care

Peas can be sown outdoors in April, and although I sow mine undercover, I make a direct sowing of peas in August. By the time the plants from this second sowing are in flower, the pea moth is no longer active (see Garden tip).

For outdoor sowings, I dig a narrow trench, 6in (15cm) wide and 2in (5cm) deep, creating ridges of soil on either side of the trench. The seeds are sown at 2in (5cm) intervals along both outer edges of the trench, just inside the ridges of soil. After marking the start and end of each row with a short cane, I backfill with the soil from the ridges and water. Germination takes 10 days, and when the plants are around 3in (8cm) high, I'll insert spent raspberry canes for additional support, just as I did when I planted my indoor-sown peas.

As soon as flowers appear in May, I give the plants a weekly comfrey or liquid seaweed feed (see p8) as well as water them once a week. If we have a very dry spring, I'll increase the frequency of watering to two to three times per week.

From June to the end of August, the pea moth is on the wing and looking for pea flowers. By this time the flowers on my indoor-sown peas will have faded, so they won't be susceptible to attack. Peas sown outdoors in April, however, will need to be covered with fine netting from May onward, to keep the insects out.

Harvesting

Peas are ready to pick around six weeks after the flowers have faded, and I can harvest my early sown pods in late June, knowing they won't have been nibbled by pests. The peas I sowed outdoors in August have flowers by mid-September, when the pea moth is no longer flying, and I can be picking healthy pods (and munching fresh peas) around the end of October.

Kitchen tip

Although my family isn't keen on peas, I manage to smuggle them into family meals when I make kachori, a delicious Gujarati dumpling-like filled pastry. It's packed with crushed peas perked up with chopped chiles, grated ginger, and an array of spices. Certainly tickles their taste buds!

STRAWBERRY

Fragaria x ananassa

For many people, strawberries signal the arrival of summer, but when I took over the plot and saw just how many strawberry plants were growing there, I didn't know whether to be happy or horrified—there are only so many fresh strawberries a family can eat! After a good harvest that summer, I didn't want to waste the fruit, so there was only one thing for it: I had to take up the challenge and overcome my fear of making jam. Nowadays, I quite enjoy dabbling in a range of preserves, and even take part in competitions. And this is all thanks to those first strawberry plants on the plot.

Understanding strawberry types

Summer-fruiting varieties produce the largest fruits. Although their season is short, growing a mix of early-, mid-, and late-fruiting types will ensure a steady supply. By comparison, perpetual strawberries are small but delicious, and my favorites. The size of each harvest is

Rekha's favorites

'Cambridge Favourite' (early)
'Honeoye' (mid)
'Mara des Bois' (perpetual)

also small, but the plants will crop through summer until the first fall frost. Alpine strawberries, the third type, bear tiny fruits that are aromatic and sweet. They are very easy to grow and tolerate shade and cool conditions.

Starting off

The early-fruiting plants I inherited in the plot stopped cropping well and were soon exhausted. Consequently, when I discovered strawberries produce the best fruit in year two and need replacing after year three, I decided to start again with some new bare-root plants. Available in winter, when dormant, these are the best value. You will also get free plantlets from them (see p110).

I prop up new bare-root plants in a bucket, adding enough water to cover the roots, then leave them overnight. The next day I mix peat-free potting mix with a handful of blood and bone meal fertilizer and pot them in troughs or 2 pint (1 liter) containers, making sure the central crown is above the soil level. After firming and watering them, I transfer the plants to the unheated greenhouse.

Above Strawberry flowers, as on this 'Honeoye' variety, are usually white with yellow centers.

Below Pick when the fruits are red all over. They will keep for two days in the fridge.

Above Strawberries reproduce with runners. Wait until year two before potting them to make new plants.

Below My plantlets are nestled into troughs in early fall and will bear fruit next summer.

By March, when new growth emerges from the central crown, I move the strawberry plants to a sheltered spot outdoors, watering if the soil feels dry. Three weeks later, the troughs move to their final position, raised up on the back of my pallet bench in full sun.

Free plants

Over time, strawberry plants will repay your care by producing plantlets (baby plants), on long, stemlike runners, which can be potted to create more plants. Runners emerge in summer, in both the plant's first and second years, but I don't recommend using first-year runners to create new plants. These take energy and nutrients from the "mother" plant and prevent it from getting fully established, so I cut them off.

Along each runner are small clumps of leaf and roots, each a plant in the making, and I retain only the strongest-looking one on each runner. With my chosen plantlet still attached, I carefully nestle it into a 2¾in (7cm) pot of potting mix, ensuring the crown is above the soil. To weigh the runner down and ensure the roots are making good contact with the mix, I cover the surface with fine gravel, water, and keep the pots in an upright position.

As soon as I notice more leaf growth and see roots coming out through the drainage hole (usually after 4–6 weeks), I sever the runner—the umbilical cord—and the baby strawberry plant is born! The next stage is to move the small plants to a sheltered area and repot them into larger 3½in (9cm) pots. I also snip off any flowers so the plants' energy is focused on putting down roots, and keep them well-watered. In September, the plants go into the troughs and are hardy enough to stay outside over winter.

Routine care

When you grow strawberries in containers, you must never allow the potting mix to dry out. Over the summer I tend to water twice a day as the plants are in full sun. I also avoid watering from overhead because if the crown and leaves of the plant remain wet, the fungal disease botrytis (gray mold) can strike. Then, as soon as flowers form, I'll start a weekly high-potash feed of diluted liquid seaweed or comfrey, again watering at ground level to prevent gray mold from forming on the fruit. Removing decaying leaves and fruit promptly will also minimize the spread of disease. Finally, for good-sized fruits, always keep your pots weed-free.

Harvesting

Strawberry flowers are fragrant and, even better, bees love them. Depending on the variety, fruits will form in mid-June soon after the flowers have been pollinated, and with a good watering and feeding regimen in place, they increase in size within a couple of weeks. Sometimes, I snip off any leaves that are shading the fruit to let in more sunlight and hasten ripening. When the fruits are red all over, it's time for harvesting; I recommend snipping or pinching the stalk to pick the fruit rather than pulling. This way, you won't risk damaging the soft berries.

Garden tip

I used to plant strawberries in a bed in the plot, but no matter how much protection I provided from slugs, the pests always managed to spoil the fruit. Now I grow my plants in terracotta troughs so that the fruit is raised off the ground. There is much less damage, any slugs are easily picked off and disposed of, and the dangling fruit is a very pretty sight.

Below A mulch of straw around the plants holds moisture in the soil and suppresses weeds.

Kitchen tip

I love making strawberry jam, but I'll also dry thin slices of the fresh fruit in a low oven to make strawberry-flake cupcakes. Fold a handful into your cupcake batter, reserving a few to put on the top. I can guarantee these fruit cupcakes will not have soggy bottoms!

SPINACH

Spinacia oleracea

I've never heard anything exciting said about spinach, but on the other hand this unassuming green leaf is very dependable—a bit like the family member who is there in the background at every gathering.

Delicate-flavored and versatile, spinach plays a vital role in my kitchen and is a permanent fixture of my summer vegetable bed. I also grow it as a cut-and-come again crop, adding the young, ground-hugging leaves to salads through the cooler months.

The cartoon character "Popeye," who loved spinach, may have motivated me to eat it when I was a child. Now, I flavor the wilted leaves with nutmeg, adding a drizzle of oil. Coincidentally, "Olive Oyl" was Popeye's girlfriend!

Rekha's favorites

'Blight Resistant Virginia'
'Bloomsdale Longstanding'
Spinach 'Perpetual'

Sowing and container growing

I sow spinach in March in cell trays at a depth of 1–1¼in (2.5–3cm), covering the seeds with a fine layer of sieved compost. After watering using a can with a fine rose, I keep the trays in the greenhouse.

By early April, the seedlings are ready to be pricked out into 2¾in (7cm) pots. When they have developed 3–5 true leaves, I transfer the pots into the cold frame to start the hardening-off process (see p152).

In addition to sowing spinach under cover, I also sow it in containers. The seeds are scattered thinly on the surface of firmed potting mix in troughs and medium-sized pots, where the plants will spend the whole growing season. You can also sow spinach direct in March, in shallow drills at a depth of ¾in (2cm). It isn't necessary to thin the plants once they have germinated.

Below Spinach is best harvested young, while the leaves are still fresh and tender.

Top While I'm
hand-weeding
spinach, I check
the leaves for signs
of pest attack.

Opposite right
Young spinach leaves
are full of nutrients.
I pick them regularly
and add to salads.

Garden tip

I also grow perpetual spinach,
a member of the beet family,
with coarser leaves and stems
than "true" spinach. It is sown,
repotted, and planted outside
in exactly the same way. As
long as I don't pick too many
leaves, perpetual spinach will
keep producing right through
fall and winter.

Planting outside

Spinach has one important requirement: it must be kept
cool, so grow it in a bright spot, but one that is out of the
hot midday sun. Around mid-April, the hardened-off
spinach seedlings are planted outside in rows in the
brassica bed, which I've already prepped by digging in
farm manure and straw to help retain moisture in the soil
over the summer months. I space the plants 12in (30cm)
apart and always make sure each planting hole is at least
6cm (15cm) deep, which helps anchor the root system. I
also leave 6in (15cm) between each row. Before watering,
I firm the soil in well around the plants so that the wind
doesn't rock the stems, which will reach a maximum
height of 8in (20cm), later in the season. Wind-rock
would cause the spinach to bolt (flower prematurely)
and compromise the harvest.

Routine care

Spinach, as I've already emphasized, needs regular
watering, especially during hot, dry periods, and I never
let the soil dry out. Also, keep a lookout for pale-green
blotches on the leaves—a sure sign that the larvae of the
beet leaf miner is munching away under the leaf surface.
You may be able to squash and kill the maggots inside the
leaf; otherwise, remove affected leaves—as well as other
dead foliage and debris close to the plants—to prevent
the pest from overwintering in the soil.

Kitchen tip

Mature spinach leaves make the best substitute for mustard greens in the famous spicy Punjabi vegetarian dish, saag paneer. Sauté diced onions with green chile, grated ginger, and garlic. Then add chili, cumin powder, and plenty of garam masala, followed by freshly chopped tomatoes. Pack the pan with spinach and a little water, let the greens wilt, then blend until smooth. Return to the pan, add the paneer cheese and a little cream, and then serve with rice. Enjoy!

Harvesting

Young, tender spinach leaves can be harvested just six weeks after germination, when they are no more than 2½in (6cm) long. Containers are very practical for growing these baby leaves because they are easier to access and harvest from pots and troughs.

I pick mature spinach leaves from May to the end of June, while they are still edible and haven't become too coarse or bitter-tasting. I tend to harvest the leaves in large amounts and then take them home to process and cook in batches. Any leaves that aren't used fresh, I wash and wilt in a steamer. After squeezing out excess moisture, they are divided into portions and stored in the freezer for later use. They taste fantastic in fish pie.

DILL

Anethum graveolens

To say dill is my favorite herb would be something of an understatement. I love the whole plant—leaves, flowers, and seeds. The filigree foliage adds depth to all my grilled or roasted seafood dishes, and I am passionate about making my own gravlax (raw salmon cured with salt and sugar and then flavored with dill). And have you tried dill-flower tea? It's a subtle stomach soother.

But to me, the seeds that follow are particularly precious. I use them in all my brines when I'm pickling vegetables, including gherkins (see p60), and a little goes a long way as I learned when I overdid the quantities for one batch! As an experiment, I've also added crushed dill seeds to a fish pie, which tasted amazing. This fantastic herb will definitely find its way into more of my dishes.

Rekha's favorites

'Dukat'
'Mammoth'
'Nano'

Sowing

Seed packets suggest sowing dill seed in cells before repotting, but this disturbs the developing roots and I've had better results sowing direct. In early May, I dig in

Top Dill dislikes being buffeted by gusts of wind, so I add a simple support.

Bottom Tiny, yellow-green dill flowers bloom in flat-topped clusters, called umbels.

compost and straw to the growing area to enrich the soil and help retain moisture. Then after raking to create a fine tilth, I cover the soil with an insulating layer of horticultural fleece. On the day before sowing, I water using a fine rose attachment if the soil feels dry, then re-cover with fleece.

The next morning, after incorporating a handful of blood and bone meal fertilizer, I scatter the dill seeds (see Garden tip), then rake over the soil very lightly. It's not necessary to bury such small seeds. Watering and setting a beer trap are next (see p10)—slugs like dill as much as I do—then I put back the fleece again. In less than a week, seedlings appear. I remove the fleece and water regularly.

When the plants are about 4in (10cm) tall, I pinch off the tops and use the feathery leaves in the kitchen. This also triggers growth from side shoots further down the stem, so it's a win-win strategy. When the plants are 12in (30cm) tall, I also enclose them with a support of canes and twine. Dill can grow to over 3ft (1m) and the support helps to keep the plants upright in windy spells.

Harvesting

From late May, I pick the top growth, which thickens up the plants, then continue harvesting through June and July when the plants are in bloom. It's a joy to see the flowers attracting so many pollinators. Seedheads follow and I harvest them by the end of August, spreading the seeds out in the potting shed to dry out fully before storing them at home. Happy summer memories in a jar.

Garden tip

Instead of sowing dill in neat rows, I prefer to scatter the seeds in their growing area. As the seedlings put on feathery growth, they help prop each other up.

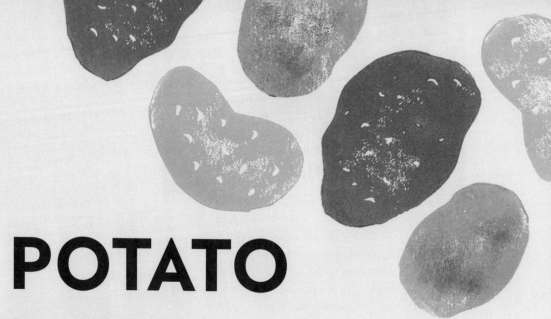

POTATO

Solanum tuberosum

Gardeners say that once you've grown and eaten your first homegrown spuds, the taste never leaves you. This proved very true in my case. I grew 'Charlotte' (a midseason variety) in a pot in the back garden, and harvesting them felt like sifting for nuggets of gold. Too excited to count them, I still remember those perfect, egg-sized potatoes and how much we all enjoyed them that evening. Unlike store-bought varieties, these weren't just fillers; they had a real flavor, and I was hooked.

Later, when I took on my half-plot at the allotment, I couldn't wait for spring to arrive so that I could plant potatoes in the ground! And with so many modern and heirloom varieties available, I had so many choices. I soon learned that if I planted all three types—early season, midseason, and late season—we could be eating delicious homegrown potatoes for most of the year.

Starting off seed potatoes

Before planting my seed potatoes, which I buy so that I know they are certified disease-free, I prefer to "chit" them

Rekha's favorites

Early season potatoes
'Red Duke of York'
'Swift'

Midseason potatoes
'Charlotte'
'Kestrel'

Late-season potatoes
'Desiree'
'International Kidney'
'King Edward'

them (encourage them to sprout), by arranging them in a layer on trays or in empty egg cartons. I tend to do this in January and set them out either in the greenhouse or on a cool windowsill in the house. The process of chitting potatoes not only gives the tubers a head start by encouraging faster growth, it also reassures me that what I've put into the ground will be viable. When the small, dark chits (shoots) that form on the tubers after about six weeks are about ½in (1cm) long, they can be planted outside, although the timing will depend on the type.

Understanding potato types

Potatoes are grouped according to when they are ready to harvest. Early season potatoes,are the first to mature, taking just 10 to 12 weeks from planting outside. Small in size, they're ideal for tight spaces or for growing in pots. After these come midseason potatoes, which take 14 to 16 weeks to mature. Late-season potatoes are the last to be planted, and take 16 to 22 weeks to mature. With thicker skins than the other two types, they can be left in the ground for longer and also store well.

Preparing the soil

To prepare the ground for planting early season potatoes, I start in February (weather permitting) by turning the soil, scattering pelleted chicken manure over it, then lightly raking and leveling the area. Worms, which are drawn to chicken manure, help break down the soil, and their casts (a.k.a. worm poo) add organic fertilizer for free. Next, I lay horticultural fleece over the ground, leaving it in place for the next 3–4 weeks to help warm up the soil.

Planting outside

Between mid- and late March I dig a trench 12in (30cm) deep, add a 6in-(15cm-) layer of well-rotted compost to the base, and top this with a very thin layer of soil that my early season seed potatoes will sit on. Carefully placing

Top Given good light and a cool spot, seed potatoes will produce dark, healthy chits.

Above If you are short on space, grow early season potatoes in a sack and remember to keep earthing them up.

Right I leave enough space between potato rows for a plank, which spreads my weight while I earth up the plants.

Bottom Potatoes keep you guessing. Until you dig up the plant, the size of the harvest is unknown.

Opposite right Yellow-fleshed potatoes seem to last particularly well in storage.

Garden tip

Sporadic watering of potatoes is something I frown upon. Not only does it lead to uneven tuber growth, but also to splits in the tubers. This usually happens when the soil has dried out and the plant has taken up an excessive amount of water. Potatoes are thirsty plants and need to be kept moist when in full leaf, so water weekly, and even twice weekly in dry weather.

the potatoes 8–12in (20–30cm) apart with the chits upright, I mark the trench at either end to identify the row, then backfill gently with the remaining soil, taking care not to dislodge the tuber or break the chits. Once one trench is completed, I move on to the next, allowing 24in (60cm) between rows for first earlies. After watering, using a can with a fine rose attachment, I replace the fleece and keep checking for green shoots to appear over the next week to two weeks. When this happens, I remove the fleece during the day, replacing it at night in case temperatures drop.

Earthing up and routine care
As soon as there's about 4in (10cm) of growth above ground, I'll earth up my early potatoes by drawing soil from both sides of the trench with a rake to almost cover the tops, leaving just 2–3 leaves exposed. Back goes the fleece, which is kept in place overnight until the last frost (around mid-May). As the plants grow taller, I continue to earth up. Potatoes are produced on the stem rather than the roots, so drawing soil up and over the stem helps trigger the production of tubers. Earthing up also stops them from turning green and inedible, and keeps the plants upright. It's also very important to water potatoes regularly, never letting the soil dry out (see Garden tip, left).

Midseason potatoes are grown in the same way as early season, with the same planting distances and depth, but are planted outside a month later. Late season seed potatoes go into the ground last, in early May, with a wider spacing than early and midseason, and 30in (75cm) between rows. Planting them 16in (40cm) apart and 6in (15cm) deep will allow the tubers to grow bigger; it's this crop that will feed us through the winter.

Harvesting

Ten weeks after planting outside, around mid-June, early seasons will be flowering—a sure sign that potatoes have formed below and are ready for harvesting. Early seasons are best eaten when freshly dug because their thin skins mean they don't store well. I tend to dig up a couple of plants at a time, as needed, through June and July. midseasons flower about a month later than early seasons, around mid-July, but are harvested and used in the same way.

Harvesting late-season potatoes is slightly different. When flowers emerge in August, I continue to earth up and water regularly, but as soon as the flowers turn into fruits, I snip these off so all the plant's energy goes into the tubers. By late August, as the leaves yellow, I stop watering and remove the top growth to within 6in (15cm) of the base. This accelerates skin hardening on the tubers. Three weeks later, from mid-September onward, it's time to dig up the crop, and I choose a dry day.

Storing late-season potatoes

First, I lay out the plants in the fall sunshine to dry out any clumps of soil still attached to the tubers. A few hours later, I brush these clumps off. Never wash potatoes because any bacteria in the water can spoil the tubers. After inspecting the harvest, I remove any soft or slug-damaged tubers, then store my crop in brown burlap sacks in a cool garage or shed for winter use.

CHIVES

Allium schoenoprasum

I grew this perennial herb from seed once, over ten years ago. Since then, chives have continued to flower and self-seed all over the plot, even between the paving slabs outside the greenhouse and in the mulch paths. I've never had to sow seeds again, and all the seeds I gather when the pretty lilac-pink flowers fade are destined for homemade naan. They make the perfect substitute for kalonji (nigella seeds).

The fresh leaves have a milder onion flavor than those of other alliums, and in summer they appear in my family's most requested dish—potato salad. I love them finely chopped in cheese, chili, and chive scones—served warm and always with a cup of masala chai!

Rekha's favorites

Garlic chives
Siberian chives

Sowing and dividing

Sow chive seeds outdoors in early fall where you want them to grow. I scattered my first seeds in the herb bed and covered them with a layer of sieved garden soil. I didn't even water them; the fall rain did that for me. Those

seeds stayed dormant until the start of the following spring when I noticed little grasslike blades. By April, the plants had developed into a lovely, lush-green clump.

Growing and harvesting

Chives are said to prefer fertile, moist soil. The self-seeded plants in the plot seem to manage fine without additional moisture, but my main clump in the herb bed, which is watered regularly, produces healthier and more vigorous growth. I like to harvest the leaves, which I snip off above the base of the stem, for an early harvest, just before the flower stalks are produced in May. Soon enough I will get a second flush of leaves that I harvest through June, as I need them. By July, I let the plant produce flower buds, which I pick just before they open. These nectar-rich buds are brought home, air-dried, and stored in airtight containers to add to homemade cheese biscuits.

Garden tip

Letting chives flower around your growing area will attract not only bees, but also aphid predators, such as hoverflies and ladybugs. Chives planted near carrots can also help mask the smell of the foliage and deter the carrot root fly. But if you don't want chives to self-seed in your vegetable bed, remove the flowers before they go to seed.

Above I like to replant clumps of self-sown chives around the plot to help with pest control.

Below far left As well as regular chives, I grow blue–mauve flowered Siberian chives, and also garlic chives for their delicate flavor.

Below left Leave some pompom heads for pollinators, but snip off a few to add fresh to summer salads.

125

CILANTRO

Coriandrum sativum

Some people love it, others hate it, but powerful, punchy cilantro is the one herb I cannot do without. A staple in my mother's kitchen and essential in Asian cooking, cilantro is part of my culinary heritage and was the first herb I grew on the windowsill. It's one of the easiest herbs to grow from seed and is happy in a container outdoors, as long as you keep it in a partially shaded spot out of direct sun, water it regularly, and bring the pot under cover in the cooler months.

After harvesting the fresh green leaves, I leave the plant to flower and it becomes a magnet for hoverflies. The round, spicy coriander seeds soon follow and I love to dry, crush, and use them in a variety of dishes including onion bhajiya (please don't say bhaaji, that's incorrect!). I also add whole seeds to brines for pickles and preserves.

Rekha's favorites

'Confetti'
'Leisure'
'Santo'

Sowing

I make three sowings of cilantro over the growing season, starting in March when I sow under cover in the greenhouse (a light windowsill also works well). After soaking the seeds overnight, I sow a single seed per cell in peat-free seed-starting mix, then cover with ½in (1cm) of sieved compost. I don't start off seeds in seed trays because thinning and transplanting at this early stage causes root disturbance. After germinating 7–10 days later, the seedlings grow quickly, and when each has a good root system, I transplant them into a 5-pint (3-liter) pot with some crocks in the bottom. By mid-May, I move the container outdoors to a sheltered, partially shaded spot. As the weather warms, I ensure the potting mix is kept moist, and always water from the base.

My second and third sowings are made direct. In May, I sow cilantro near my transplanted celeriac, and the July seeds go into the area where my early peas grew (see pp104–107) to take advantage of the nutritious nitrogen this crop left behind in the soil. I sow seeds in a patch, rather than a row (see Dill, pp116–17). This arrangement helps the growing plants support and protect each other—a tip I learned from small-scale farmers in India.

Harvesting

Once the plants are about 4in (10cm) tall, I cut off the top 2¾in (7cm) to promote leafy growth farther down. New shoots will soon appear from the center, which I leave to grow. When the plants are 6in (15cm) high, I pick leaves from half of them. Two weeks later, I do the same with the remaining plants and notice that the plants in the first section I harvested have put on substantial growth. I could sow on a succession basis every three weeks and harvest whole plants, but I much prefer picking the outer leaves of established plants, which continue to produce leaves with a strong flavor.

By August I will let some of the March-sown plants flower and go to seed, which I collect when it is pale brown and ripe. I save some dried coriander seed for next year's sowing, and the rest is put to good use in the kitchen.

Above To protect them against frost, tender cilantro seedlings are repotted and kept under cover until mid-May.

Below Grown in semi-shade and watered well, cilantro is less likely to bolt.

MINT

Mentha

When I discovered just how many varieties of this popular herb were available, it was enough to make my head spin. There are more than 120 different types, and I was making do with just spearmint and peppermint! Admittedly, these are my go-to mints for most of the year, but I have a small collection, including chocolate and Moroccan mints, that I like to show off to visiting gardeners. There is also a variegated variety, but I've yet to get my hands on it.

Growing from cuttings

I've tried growing mint from seed, but without success. It is far easier to propagate from cuttings when the plant is in leaf but before it flowers, and I've found late spring is the best time to take them. Cut off a piece of stem, about 4in (10cm) long, remove the lower leaves, and insert in a 3½in (9cm) pot of damp potting mix. Leave the potted cutting in a greenhouse or outside in a bright, sheltered spot out of direct sun, and by midsummer the roots will have filled the pot. At this stage, you can transfer the mint

Rekha's favorites

'Chocolate'
Moroccan
Peppermint
Spearmint

into a large terracotta pot and put it in a partially shaded spot, as I do in the garden at home. If you're tempted to plant it straight into the ground, be warned: mint is a rampant herb, and its spreading roots will colonize space very quickly. In the allotment, I first planted my mint in a plastic pot with the bottom cut out, then sank this pot into the herb bed. The pot creates a barrier, keeping the roots under control. I grow mint in full sun in the plot, and it doesn't complain, but I do provide plenty of moisture and never let it dry out.

Harvesting

You can pick mint from early spring when new growth appears, then cut back the plants in summer to promote new growth. I tend to harvest peppermint and spearmint stems in late spring so that I can dry them in the potting shed, and then use the dried, crushed leaves in cooking over winter. After cutting back, a liquid seaweed or comfrey feed will give the plant a boost, and you can pick new leaves in about six weeks until the first frosts.

Top In spring, pot-grown mint produces plenty of fresh growth that make ideal cuttings.

Above Push the lower half of the mint stem into the mix around the edge of the pot and keep it well watered.

Left In spring and summer, I use freshly picked mint in cooking, but always harvest plenty of stems to dry and use in the colder months.

Garden tip

I recommend growing this highly aromatic plant near carrots and cabbages. The strong-smelling oils in the mint leaves will help keep pests away from these crops. And if you let the plant flower, the small blooms will attract pollinating insects.

BEETS

Beta vulgaris

Beets may not usually inspire passion, but for me, this vegetable is a quiet winner. Like a big brother who's got my back, beets are always there to provide me with a harvest. Winters are mild in my area, so I can grow and pick fresh beets right up until mid-November. For the rest of the year, we eat our way through the jars of pickled beets that I squirrelled away back in late August. This root doesn't ask for much when growing; and, even better, slugs avoid it. It's the perfect vegetable for first-time gardeners, thriving in almost all soil types including my clay loam, and even comfortable in pots and window boxes. But one thing beets hate is being overshadowed by the foliage of other plants, so I make sure my beets have the right kind of neighbors—namely other low-growing root crops such as turnips.

Rekha's favorites

'Burpees Golden' (yellow)
'Chioggia' (candy-striped)
'Detroit 2' (red)

Sowing and thinning

I resist the urge to sow beets direct in March. The seeds will only sulk in the lukewarm soil and may not even

germinate. By early April, the soil is warmer and well prepped after I've dug, weeded, and raked it to a fine tilth, and worked in a scattering of slow-release organic fertilizer. I'll even water the day before sowing if the soil is on the dry side because the moisture will help the seed swell and germinate successfully.

From April onward, I sow a short 12in (30cm) row of beets every month (known as succession sowing) in a very shallow drill, no more than ½in (1cm) deep. I'm a little strict when it comes to sowing, and rather than sprinkling, I carefully place the seed at 1¼–1½in (3–4cm) intervals. Each seed is actually a cluster of two or three, so being meticulous now will save time when I come to thin out the seeds in three weeks. By then, my to-do list will be as long as my arm!

Once the seeds are sown and covered with soil, I tap down the row with the back of a trowel so that the seeds

Top Whether you choose striped, orange, or plain red varieties, beets are an easy crop to grow.

Bottom Some gardeners presoak beet seeds, but this isn't necessary if you water well after sowing.

make good contact and any air pockets are removed. I then water using a can with a fine rose attachment. After germination (which can take 7–10 days), I'll wait for true leaves to appear before thinning the seedlings, spacing them according to the variety and how large I want the beets to grow. Just 2in (5cm) between seedlings is perfect for the blood-red varieties, which I prefer to harvest at golf-ball size so that I can tuck more whole roots into a jar when pickling. Any remaining beets are left to grow to tennis-ball size, which will be delicious roasted. When thinning seedlings of yellow and candy-striped beets, I allow a spacing of 2½in (6cm), and harvest them when tennis-ball size, ready to use raw or roasted.

Routine care

Beets are not needy, but they appreciate a weekly watering and weeding so that the fattening roots aren't left to compete with weeds for food and moisture. The rounded tops of the roots are soon visible above the soil, so always weed around them with care.

In summer, I look out for irregular blotches on the leaves that look like scorch marks, but which soon turn brown and shrivel. This isn't natural wilting, which would continue up the whole leaf, but damage by a pest—the beet leaf miner. The larvae of this fly burrow under the leaf surface, creating distinct grooves, but I stop any further damage by squashing the grubs and burning affected leaves.

Garden tip

When thinning beets, I place the tips of my index and middle fingers on either side of the seedling I'd like to keep. This ensures that the soil around it isn't disturbed when I pull out its unwanted neighbors. These spare seedlings aren't wasted. I take them back to the kitchen, where they make a great, tasty addition to salads.

Harvesting

Beets are usually ready to harvest 10–15 weeks after sowing. My first sowing in April will be ready in mid-June, and I simply grab all the leaves and gently pull up the half-protruding roots. No need to use a trowel. A short sowing each month until August will see me pulling beets into November—but given that it's more than 15 weeks since the last rows were sown, I know I will probably be harvesting some monsters!

Above Spacing red varieties closely, stops the roots from growing too large.

Left Fresh beets don't store well, so harvest only as many roots as you need.

Opposite Freshly thinned beet seedlings taste good in salads or stir-fries.

Kitchen tip

Freshly pulled beets, especially the candy-striped varieties, are fantastic grated and eaten raw in salads. The mellow flavor of yellow-fleshed beets, however, really comes through when they are roasted in the oven. After peeling the cooked beets, I chop them into chunks, add a few steamed edamame beans, then toss everything together in a tahini dressing. There will be no leftovers, I promise!

FALL

This is the season when baskets and burlap sacks are packed with produce, and jars of preserved vegetables line pantry shelves. Fall is a time to be thankful.

APPLE

Malus domestica

"Ooh, it looks just like the one in the Ladybird books!", I said when my mom first gave a bright red apple to each of us children back in Zambia, where I was brought up. Such a pretty fruit, but the taste was a real disappointment. These imported eating apples had probably spent so long in refrigerated storage that they had lost their flavor and crisp texture. I know now that the dry, mealy apple was 'Red Delicious', but had no idea so many other varieties existed until, years later, I visited a local London vegetable market as an adult. My eyes lit up as a whole new world of apples revealed itself and, with so many old and heirloom varieties making a comeback, I still can't say which is my favorite. Yet I knew one thing for sure: I wanted to grow an apple tree in my allotment. But which one?

Rekha's favorites

'Beauty of Bath' (early)
'Braeburn' (late)
'Elstar' (patio variety)
'Gala' (mid)

Choosing the right tree

I wanted a tree that produced eating rather than cooking apples, and a variety suited to the conditions on my plot. Its eventual size was also a major factor

138

because a large, spreading tree would cast its shade over my precious vegetables. With apple trees, this size is determined by the part growing beneath the soil (the rootstock), and my small tree was grown on a dwarfing rootstock. I'm also scared of heights—another reason for choosing a small tree. Mine will reach no more than 10ft (3m), and I can reach and pick the fruit using a small, three-step ladder.

I also kept in mind that planting a tree is not just for the here and now. One day I'll leave the allotment, and I want the next plot-holders to enjoy the fruits, too.

Planting the tree

Apple trees need a sunny, sheltered spot (south- or southwest-facing is best) to produce a good harvest. For protection, I planted mine close to the greenhouse and shed, where it was out of the wind. Strong gusts can

Garden tip

The most cost-effective way to buy an apple tree is to choose a bare-root "whip." These are very young trees, dug up from the ground and sold with no soil around their roots. They are available during their dormant season from late fall to winter. I went for a two-year-old apple whip, and although it didn't look very attractive, mine cost less than half the price of a pot-grown tree. But don't worry if you've missed the bare-root season. You can buy container-grown apple trees year-round.

Far left Blossom appears in mid-spring and can be damaged by frost. In cold regions, choose a late-flowering apple tree.

Left Following successful pollination of the flowers on the short spurs (see p140), small fruits soon begin to swell.

destroy delicate spring blossom, or blow insects off course before they've done their vital pollinating business.

I made sure the planting hole for my bare-root tree was twice the size of the rootball, then added plenty of good-quality potting mix up to just below the swollen part of the stem. Don't bury this part, or you risk secondary roots sprouting from it and weakening growth. If you are planting a container-grown tree, it should be at the same depth it was in the pot.

Routine care

A layer of mulch in spring is so important for fruit trees. From March to April, I water the ground if the weather has been dry, then spread 2in (5cm) of homemade compost or leafmold around (but not up to) the base to make a circle 16–20in (40–50cm) in diameter. This provides much-needed nutrients in spring and helps lock in moisture and keep down weeds. In hot summer weather, I water my young tree weekly, using a watering can rather than a hose so that I know how much I've given the tree: a full can, holding 2 gallons (10 liters), should be enough.

Pruning

Fruit trees must be pruned to keep them healthy and productive, but this doesn't mean anxiously snipping off bits to give the tree a light trim for fear of killing it! There is a process to follow, and the best time to do this is winter, when the tree is dormant. But before making the first cut, I clean and sharpen my tools: pruners for thin shoots, loppers for branches up to 1½in (4cm) in diameter, and a small pruning saw for any growth that is thicker than this.

On each branch, I locate the short spurs (growing points) that will bear flowers and fruit and make a note of the 3–4 strongest-looking ones. The rest are removed, with a clean cut above an outward-facing spur. The next task is to remove any branches that are crossing because they will rub and create wounds where disease can enter. It's also a good idea to prune branches that are growing into the center of the tree. This opens it up and increases airflow to help keep disease at bay, as well as allows more sunlight to reach the fruits.

Harvesting

Apples ripen at different times, from early-season fruits that can be picked and eaten in late summer to late-season varieties that ripen in October. I harvest my apples in September, when the fruits are a good color and come away easily with the stalk attached. I'm always careful not to drop my apples, or they'll bruise and won't store well.

Above left When leaves and blossom appear, it's time to hang up a sticky trap for natural pest control (see Garden tip).

Above During the "June drop," some apples will fall naturally from the clusters, which helps thin them out.

Bottom Pick apples by gently cupping the fruit in your palm, then giving it a light twist.

Garden tip

Apples are magnets for a particular pest: the small codling moth. The females lay eggs in early summer and the caterpillars burrow into and eat the developing fruit. The first time I harvested my apples, I noticed the tiny entry and exit holes, but when the apples were cut open they had brown, rotten patches. I now buy pheromone traps to hang in the tree in early spring. These sticky traps attract and catch the male moth before it can get anywhere near the female.

RASPBERRY

Rubus idaeus

When I took over the plot from John, the previous owner, I was overjoyed to discover I had inherited raspberry canes. Raspberries are perennial plants and there are two types, summer- and fall-fruiters; John's were the summer-fruiting variety. Unfortunately, my jubilation proved to be short-lived. The plants looked weary, and even after a lot of TLC—I fed the soil with chicken manure and bonemeal, and added plenty of mulch—they sulked. Sadly, after two seasons I had to take them out (sorry, John!). But the fall-fruiting canes I replaced them with established well in just two years, and they provide me with the most delicious, fragrant berries I have ever tasted.

Choosing the variety

Having grown both summer- and fall-fruiting raspberries, I can tell you the fall-fruiting types crop more heavily, are far easier to take care of, and even do well in large pots. Summer-fruiters can grow up to 5ft (1.5m), and the lanky, top-heavy canes need the support of posts and horizontal

Rekha's favorites

'All Gold'
'Autumn Bliss'
'Polka'

Left All fall-fruiting raspberries freeze well, especially the smaller-fruited varieties.

wires. In September, after harvesting, canes that have finished fruiting must be removed and new season's growth meticulously tied in to the supports. With only a small, dedicated fruit section on my plot and limited time to care for it given how many vegetables I grow, I realized fall-fruiting raspberries would be less labor-intensive than summer-fruiters. And although their fruits might be smaller, fall-fruiters would give me a bigger harvest. So, the summer fruiters had to go and this section covers only fall-fruiting types. I was given these as bare-root canes (with no soil attached) by another gardener, and would have chosen these over pot-grown fruit as they are much cheaper.

Planting outside

Bare-root, fall-fruiting canes are available to buy from November to February, when the plants are dormant. At this time of year with many of the beds on the plot cleared, I had a better idea of the space and could find a planting spot for the canes that was exactly right. When I planted mine in early winter, the soil hadn't yet frozen, so I worked in several scoops of manure (compost also works

well) when I filled each planting hole, to provide an extra
boost of nutrients when the raspberry canes woke up the
following spring. I allowed about 2ft (60cm) between
each cane to give the new shoots that emerge from the
soil plenty of space to grow. Once planted (see Garden
tip, below), I cut the existing canes down to 12in (30cm).
This sounds drastic, but it helps the new plants
concentrate their energy into making good roots so
that they establish well.

Pruning and routine care

Each January I prune all the growth on my established
raspberry canes down to 4in (10cm) from soil level.
I find it's worth keeping the spent canes—they come in
useful as supports for my peas (see pp104–107).

With the base of the canes clear, I gently scratch around
the top of the soil with a hand fork to uncover any bugs
that might be hibernating in the shelter of the foliage.
Once exposed to the cold air, the bugs will either die or
provide a welcome protein snack for visiting robins. About
four days later, I mulch around, but not right up to, the
canes with a 2in-(5cm-) layer of soil to encourage the
dormant buds on the short stems to produce new side
shoots in spring.

As new growth emerges, the mulch locks in moisture;
then in early summer I water well at least once a week.
When the canes are about 5ft (1.5 meters) tall, I create a
support for the stems well before they become heavy
with fruit, from steel fencing poles and three tiers of rope.

Garden tip

When planting bare-root
raspberry canes, look for the
small bump on the stem
closest to the roots (known as
the node) and make sure that
it's below soil level. New shoots
will emerge from this node and
grow upward and outward
come spring.

As flower buds form in midsummer, I apply a weekly seaweed feed and keep this up until late September, or until the plants have stopped fruiting. I don't net the plants against birds because the netting snags too easily and damages the berries when I take it off. But I still get a decent harvest, aided by my bird deterrent, Henry the imitation Hawk, who keeps pigeons and magpies away.

Harvesting

Although the harvest is in full swing by September, berries can ripen as early as mid-August. But if they don't come away easily, leave them for a few more days. And fall-fruiters do have one disadvantage: fine, prickly thorns. As I wade through them, murmuring "Ouch!", I remind myself that scratches are a small price to pay for the jars of raspberry jam that will soon be on my shelves. I'll also have enough to freeze, ready to add to a family favorite: a New York cheesecake, naturally with a Rekha twist!

Below, left Ripe raspberries should come away easily from their core, which stays on the plant.

Below My main harvest is in September, but in mild falls I've harvested fruit as late as November.

FLORENCE FENNEL

Foeniculum vulgare var. azoricum

Like a dancer's feathered headpiece, the tall fronds of Florence fennel seem to sway in the breeze above the swollen stem. Widely grown in its native Italy and named after its most beautiful city, this vegetable can be a bit of a diva, and what she absolutely hates is neglect. Florence fennel also likes to be tucked under a blanket of crumbly, warm soil because if this dries out for even the briefest period, she will show her disapproval by bolting—sending up umbels of white flowers. The bulb then stops swelling and is far too small to eat. Once fully grown, the taste of fennel can be a bit hit-or-miss. I've found the grated raw bulb overpowering when added to salads, but when you roast fennel slowly in the oven, its mellow, sweet, aniseed flavor really comes through.

Rekha's favorites

'Fennel de Firenze'
'Mantovano'
'Romanesco'

Sowing

I sow this heat-loving vegetable outdoors in July when the soil is warm. Although the current trend is to start fennel off in Rootrainers, I've found fennel seedlings germinate far better when sown direct. Why fuss with potting mix and containers when I can sow fennel in the space where my early potatoes were growing (see pp118–21). After lifting the potato plants, the soil texture is like breadcrumbs, which is perfect for fennel seeds. Wasting no time, I grab my rake, trowel, and stringline. First, I rake the area level, discarding any annual weeds that get caught up in the tines, then mark out a row by unrolling the string between two sticks and pulling it taut. Using the trowel to make a shallow drill no more than ½in (1cm) deep, I sow seeds at intervals of 1¼in (3cm) along the drill, then cover the seeds with the displaced soil. When that's done, I water the seeds.

Garden tip

I recommend using a can with a fine rose attachment when watering newly sown Florence fennel seeds. A heavier flow of water will just displace the seeds and they'll come up where you don't want them.

Below Thinning fennel seedlings gives the remaining stems space to swell to an edible size.

Right After thinning, keep young fennel well watered and weed free, so that all the goodness goes into producing bulbs.

Opposite By late August, the swollen stems are clearly visible. The white bulb lies just beneath soil level.

Thinning and growing

For such a fussy vegetable, fennel's germination rate can be very quick—just five to seven days in some years. When the seedlings have a pair of true leaves, I carefully thin them out, leaving a space of 2in (5cm) between each. Taken together, the width of my index, middle, and ring fingers is this exact measurement, so I use them instead of a garden ruler. Very handy!

As I mentioned, Florence fennel is a thirsty vegetable, but as long as I keep the soil moist—by watering almost every day during late summer—this beautiful vegetable is happy. I also ensure the soil around the base of the swelling stems is free from weeds. These would compete with the fennel for moisture and nutrients and I'd get smaller bulbs.

Harvesting

Fennel can be harvested as soon as the bulb has swelled to the size of an eating apple, usually around September. Rather than dig up the whole plant, I sometimes cut the bulb off just below the base and leave the roots in the soil. Within days, new growth appears from the top and the plant eventually produces a further crop before the frosts arrive. The second bulb, although slightly smaller than the first, is always a welcome bonus, especially when the seed packet indicates that you can expect only one per plant. But not if you grow fennel the Rekha way!

Depending on the weather, I can harvest fennel until November. When we have a mild winter, I have been able to gather one or two fresh bulbs into early December, provided the plants are protected from frost under a cloche. When I get home, I'll roast my Florence fennel in the oven and serve it either with some pan-fried sea bream, or chargrilled halloumi steaks. Delicious!

Garden tip

A trick I learned from a neighboring plot-holder, who happens to be Italian, is to earth up a little soil around each bulb using a hoe. This not only stops the wind from rocking the plant and causing it to bolt, but also keeps the swelling stem bases blanched and tender.

CELERIAC

Apium graveolens* var. *rapaceum

To me, this knobby, slow-growing vegetable looks almost prehistoric, and it certainly has a very long history of cultivation. Hairy and rootlike, the celeriac crown is the plant's swollen lower stem, and it likes to sit in moist soil. Yet the lovely thing about this ugly-duckling vegetable is that the whole plant (apart from the rhino-tough skin) is edible, with a subtle, celerylike flavor. I pinch off and dry the leaves to make celery salt and use the stalks in dishes as a celery substitute—they just need to be cooked a little longer. The flesh, boiled with potato, is wonderful mashed, and is also delicious roasted or made into fries.

Sowing

I had always wanted to grow celeriac and celery, but year after year, my seeds failed to germinate. I blamed this on substandard seeds and unsuitable greenhouse conditions, but honestly the fault lay with yours truly! After seven unsuccessful years, the eureka moment came when I learned that both seeds require light to germinate,

Rekha's favorites

'Giant Prague'
'Monarch'
'Prinz'

whereas I'd foolishly been covering them with mix. Oh joy! So now, in March, I fill a seed tray almost to the top with seed-starting mix, firm it, and sieve a little more mix over it to give the celeriac seeds a fine cushion to settle on. I then sow thinly and gently tamp the seeds down with my wooden tamper so that they make good contact. Next, I put the tray in water and don't remove it until the top of the mix is thoroughly damp. This can take up to half an hour. Finally, I cover the tray with a propagator lid.

Pricking out

Patience is key. Germination can take between two and four weeks, and then you need to wait for the first true celeriac leaves to appear before pricking out. When my seedlings look sturdy, I uproot them from their comfort zone and repot them into individual 2¾in (7cm) pots or 2in (5cm) cell trays filled with potting mix.

At this stage, I'll water the seedlings and give them an early boost with a very, very diluted feed of homemade

Garden tip

Celeriac seeds need plenty of daylight, as well as night-time darkness, to kick-start the germination process. I put the tray of seeds in the greenhouse (a bright windowsill indoors would also work) and make sure they don't dry out.

Right I use a wooden presser, not my hands, to level the surface of the mix before sowing.

Below Always water celeriac from the base so that the small seeds aren't displaced.

Far right When the tray has drained, cover it with a propagator lid. Warmth and humidity will aid germination.

nettle tea (see p8)—no more than 1 teaspoon of nettle concentrate to 1¾ pts (1 liter) of water. I mix this up and pour into the shallow tray that the pots are standing on. A more concentrated feed would produce too much leafy growth. From now until I plant the young celeriac outside, the soil in their pots will remain moist while they soak up sunshine in the greenhouse.

Planting outside

To lessen the shock of life outdoors, I gradually acclimatize greenhouse-raised celeriac by moving the seedlings to the cold frame come mid-April and starting the two-week hardening-off process (see p12). I also make sure the seedlings are kept well-watered during their stay.

By mid-May, when all risk of frost has passed, it's time to plant the celeriac outside in its final spot. I like to do this in a block formation, allowing 8in (20cm) between each plant. As I mentioned, this plant needs moist soil to thrive, so just before planting I fork a few handfuls of straw into the ground, which helps to retain moisture around the plants. I also keep a close eye on these plants over the summer and water twice or even three times a week so the soil never dries out.

Weeds will compete with celeriac for moisture, so I keep the growing area weed-free over the summer months. It's around this time that the white "crown"—the swollen stem—starts to form just above soil level. As it fattens, I carefully cut off those leaves that are hanging down close to the base, and I do this on a weekly basis. It not only lets in more light, but also helps the stem swell.

Harvesting

I lift my first celeriac in early September, using a garden fork. I dig the other plants up as needed because they will come to no harm if left in the ground until early December. But celeriac isn't fully hardy, so if an early frost is forecast, I make sure to mulch around the bulbous bases of the plants with straw (the tops can be left uncovered). Harvesting the first celeriac to take home and roast in the oven is a reminder that the days are getting colder and shorter.

Perfect partner: Dill

I like to scatter a few dill seeds (see pp116–17) among the celeriac seedlings and allow the mature dill plants to flower. Dill's anise-scented foliage helps stop the celery fly from attacking the celeriac, which belongs to the same family of vegetables. Tiny, yellow dill flowers also attract beneficial insects, including hoverflies, to the bed.

Opposite far left By mid-April, when I harden off the celeriac, space is at a premium in the cold frame.

Left Before planting out in a block, I unpot and lay out the young celeriac to check spacing.

Bottom left Avoided by pests but pollinator-friendly, dill is ideal for organic growers.

Below Trimming the lower leaves and watering regularly will ensure celeriac crowns swell.

SQUASH

Cucurbita moschata, Cucurbita maxima

Forget those hefty, orange Halloween pumpkins that take many months of nurturing just to be carved for one night's amusement. The squash family has much more to offer than these tasteless heavyweights, including delicious butternut as well as amazing heirloom varieties, such as Turk's turban. Thanks mainly to images shared on social media, these older types have made a comeback, and their seeds are now much more widely available. I grow a selection of squashes, both for their long storage qualities and for their taste and texture, and always use some to make a pumpkin chutney (see p157).

Rekha's favorites

'Baby Boo'
'Butternut Waltham'
'Galeux D'Eysines'
'Queensland Blue'
'Sweet Dumpling'
'Table King'

Planning and sowing

Squash needs space—up to 10ft (3m)—to accommodate the long, sprawling stem that bears several creeping side shoots. At times, I've grown the plant in a spiral by training the stem around sticks inserted every 20in (50cm), so I can accommodate three plants in a small 16ft² (5m²) space. If you don't have an area big enough, you can grow it vertically: just train the stem up a structure, such as a wooden tripod sturdy enough to take the weight of the heavy, ripe fruit. Squashes also need plenty of sunlight to grow and ripen, so don't think of planting them in shade or even part-shade. But the biggest requirement of these big, hungry plants is nutrition and water, so be prepared to feed them regularly and never, ever let them dry out.

I start off my squashes in the greenhouse in April, sowing two large, teardrop-shaped seeds at twice their depth and pointy end facing downward in individual 3½in (9cm) pots. I then remove the weaker seedling and keep it for the allotment plant sale. The growing medium I sow in has also been enriched with a couple of teaspoons of FBB fertilizer—a little trick to feed the seedling as it grows. The extra feed, and ensuring the soil stays moist, will keep the seedlings happy, allowing me to get on with all my other tasks during this busy time in the growing season.

Above In mid-May, the young squash plants move from the greenhouse to the cold frame.

Left My go-to organic method for slug control is the beer trap. Keep it topped off and the slugs will fall in.

Planting outside

Squash seedlings can be planted outdoors when there's no danger of frost. From early May, during the hardening-off period (see p12), I start prepping the soil. First, I dig in the green manure (see p18) that has been growing in the bed set aside for the squashes, followed by three to four shovels of farmyard manure and straw to make a rich mix.

When planting the young squashes, I allow at least 5ft (1.5m) between each plant so they have room to sprawl. Once planted, I give them a good soaking before putting down a beer trap (see p10) so slugs don't eat their young, tender leaves. Given such a great start in life, the plants respond by quickly putting on growth.

Routine care

Keep the soil around young squash plants moist, and water on a daily basis in warm weather. I also keep the beer trap topped off until the squash leaves develop a furry texture and prickles form along the main stem, both of which will deter slugs.

By early August, when the main stem reaches 6ft (2m) and two or three young fruits have formed, I cut off the growing tip. This forces the plant to produce side shoots, which will carry additional, smaller fruits. I grow squash every year, but seeing the swelling fruits sheltered by the broad leaves always stops me in my tracks.

Harvesting

As summer ends, the squash leaves turn from green to yellow and fall, revealing the beautiful, ripe fruits. Every September I pause to admire this perfect, curvaceous crop that has developed over the last five months. But although September can be sunny, there's often rain too, so I prevent the fruits from getting splashed and spoiled in the mud by raising them off the ground on old roof slates.

By October, before the first frosts arrive, it's time for the harvest. Using a sharp pair of pruners, I carefully cut off the fruits, always leaving a short length of stem attached, and take them into the greenhouse. After the squashes have cured (dried out completely) there for a few days, I store them at home, well spaced out on a cool, dry shelf. Squashes will keep throughout winter, but check them regularly for discolored patches. If any are spoiling, simply cut off the affected parts, then peel the squash before chopping it into chunks and freezing.

Above, right By late July, young squashes are starting to swell beneath the leaves.

Far right To aid ripening, I push aside any leaves that are shading the fruit.

Below As the name suggests, the flesh of 'Sweet Dumpling' is sweet, and a lovely orange color.

Kitchen tip

My favorite squash recipe is a chutney made with chunks drizzled in oil and roasted until just soft. I add cumin and coriander seeds, cinnamon, chopped onion, brown sugar, raisins, vinegar, and fresh orange juice to the squash, bring to a boil in a large pan, and simmer to thicken.

TURNIP

Brassica rapa (Rapifera Group)

I don't remember eating turnips as a child, but I read about them—in a Ladybird book called *The Enormous Turnip*. Then we moved to the UK, and I saw turnips in a vegetable stall and marveled at them. With purple markings at the top and a clean, white base, they seemed very small—only the size of tennis balls. Nevertheless, memories of the giant turnip came flooding back.

That was some 40 years ago. While they caught my imagination back then, I didn't think much of the taste. It was only when I got my plot—a little older and, hopefully, a little wiser—that I was keen to grow my own turnips. Now, I enjoy the spicy taste of the young leaves (turnip belongs to the cabbage family), and after cooking and eating the roots, I realize I'd missed out on a whole other taste experience when I was younger.

Sowing and pest control

To give my turnips a head start, in March I sow an early variety indoors in cell trays. By April, I feel brave enough to

Rekha's favorites

'Milan White'
'Purple Top Milan'
'Golden Ball'

sow this same variety outdoors, directly in the ground in shallow drills.

The first time I sowed turnip seed—outdoors, on a sunny day in April—my heart was jumping with excitement. Soon, I discovered that something else was jumping and making small holes in my turnip greens: flea beetles. These tiny insects decimated the foliage, which prevented me from picking and enjoying some spicy young 'Milan White' leaves for salads. When harvested, the roots hadn't developed fully, owing to the damaged foliage, and were tiny. Such a disappointment!

The next year, I learned that this pest hibernates over winter in homemade compost. So, three weeks prior to

Garden tip

Covering the turnip-growing area with horticultural insect mesh can prevent flea beetles from damaging the emerging leaves. You can also try dusting turnip seedlings with diatomaceous earth on germination. This safe and effective natural insecticide dries out the beetles' bodies. It will need reapplying after rain, but I've found that once the leaves are well established, the beetles leave them alone.

Left For "baby" turnips, sow seeds in a container indoors, in early spring.

Below I use a homemade "puffer"—a plastic bottle with holes in the cap—to apply diatomaceous earth (see Garden tip) to the seedlings.

Above Thinning direct-sown turnips gives the fast-growing roots room to swell.

Opposite, right and bottom By early winter, the last of the turnips are pulled. I cut off the leaves and stems before storing any roots.

sowing the seed, I worked my compost into the ground where the turnips would soon grow. This effectively disturbed the beetles, which were forced to flee (pardon the pun!) in search of food elsewhere. I've also learned a few other pest control techniques to keep my turnips healthy (see Garden tip, p159).

Thinning and further sowings

A couple of weeks after sowing, as the young plants grow stronger, I thin the seedlings to 4in (10cm) apart. Around the same time, I sow the next short row of seeds because turnips are quick-growing and can be sown successively right through to summer. From mid-May to August I sow 'Purple Top Milan', an heirloom variety with mild-tasting, flattish roots. Then it's time for the final sowings of late-sown varieties, including 'Golden Ball', for fall and winter harvesting. Their delicious sweetness is intensified by cold weather.

Harvesting

I could leave my turnips to grow enormous, as in my childhood book, but they would become woody, and taste like cardboard. The best time to harvest is about six weeks from sowing when the "roots" are about the size of golf balls, and definitely no bigger than a tennis ball. No need to use a fork or trowel: just grab the foliage and pull the turnips gently out of the ground.

Indoor-sown turnips that were planted outside in late March, are ready to pick from mid-April onward. After this early crop, the harvest will keep going for as long as you continue to sow turnip seed outdoors. In mild winters, I've been lucky enough to harvest late-maturing varieties in December.

Like beets, turnips store really well over winter and don't need to be spaced out on racks in a dark shed. Just keep them in wooden boxes filled with dry horticultural sand, making sure there is space between each turnip.

Kitchen tip

I like to use turnips as a potato substitute, either whole or chopped in half, in the spicy spinach curry saag aloo. To sautéed onion, grated garlic, and ginger, I add roughly chopped spinach and green turnip tops together with warming turmeric, coriander, and cumin. Next, I add some strained tomatoes, the chopped turnips, and water, then cook until tender. Serve with rice and a wedge of lemon.

WINTER

The allotment may appear to be sitting quiet and still now, but there's still work to be done: a quarter of the plot continues to produce winter greens to see me through this harsh season.

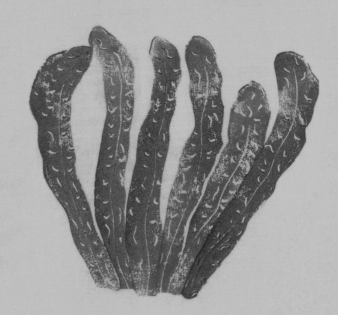

KALE

Brassica oleracea (Acephala Group)

I grow a lot of brassicas—a vegetable family that includes cabbage, Brussels sprouts, and purple sprouting broccoli—but if I had to choose just one it would be kale. This undemanding vegetable, which grows on my plot for a full 10 months of the year, withstands everything the weather can throw at it, including wet soil in winter. What's not to love? I've grown several kale varieties, from dwarf 'Red Ruble' with serrated red foliage that is excellent in salads, to 'Dazzling Blue' with blue-green crinkled leaves. However, top marks for taste go to the robust, dark-leaved Tuscan kale, 'Nero di Toscana', a.k.a. lacinato or cavolo nero.

Sowing and pricking out

In late April, once the early-spring sowing frenzy is over and there is space in the cold frame, I sow no more than 10 seeds ¾in (2cm) deep in a tray of seed-starting mix. I could start the seeds outdoors, but dare not—slugs would devour the young leaves, as would the caterpillars of cabbage white butterflies (see p30). Starting kale off

Rekha's favorites

'Dazzling Blue'
'Nero di Toscana'
'Red Ruble'

in the sheltered, north-facing cold frame not only protects the emerging seedlings from pests, but the cool environment ensures it has enough time to establish well.

Three weeks later, I prick out the seedlings into individual 2¾in (7cm) pots of potting mix and return them to the cold frame, taking the precaution of stretching fine netting over the opening before I close the lid. As the weather warms, I can keep the cold frame lid slightly open, while the netting stops cabbage whites from getting in.

Preparation and planting outside

In late April, as soon as I've sown the seeds, I start preparing the growing area for my kale by digging in the green manure that I sowed in September (see above). As it breaks down it will enrich the soil, and I also fork in a bucketful of homemade compost to preserve moisture.

By mid-May, the ground is prepped, the skies are (hopefully) blue, and my kale plants are ready for planting outdoors with 16in (40cm) space between them. The

Above, left Phacelia, a green manure, protects soil over winter. Digging it back in improves structure and adds vital nutrients.

Above When kale has formed good roots, just give the pot a gentle squeeze to remove the seedlings.

mature stems can grow up to 3ft (1m) tall, so at this stage I recommend planting the young kale 6in (15cm) deep. Although thoughts of winter aren't uppermost in my mind , I know planting deeply will anchor the kale's roots so the plants will be able to withstand strong gusts or the weight of snow. As with winter cabbage and Brussels sprouts, I then firm the plants in well and water them before putting down a beer trap (see p10). Finally, I cover the crop with a netted cloche. This is a basic tunnel cloche frame without plastic walls—it is now May, so the crop needs no extra warmth. Over this, I drape soft netting, which I then secure firmly, making sure there are no gaps. It will prevent cabbage white butterflies from getting in and laying their eggs on my young kale.

Routine care

My kale plants grow quickly, given the warm, moisture-retaining soil around their roots, and I'm soon swapping the netted cloche frame for 5ft (1.5m) bamboo poles topped by plastic bottles, with netting stretched over them. Watching me work are the local pigeons. They love all brassicas, and sit high in a nearby oak tree, waiting for me to forget to cover the crop. They clearly don't know me—I never forget!

As summer comes to an end, my early work prepping the soil is repaid by lush, crinkly green growth, and by September the kale has grown tall enough to need staking. I tie the stems to 3ft (90cm) bamboo canes to keep them upright and prevent them from being snapped by winter winds. I lift the protective netting just long enough to weed and water the plants, and spread a 2in (5cm) layer of mulch around the bases to add further goodness to the soil and help lock in moisture and warmth.

Harvesting

I have been eyeing up these super-crinkly, come-get-me leaves since August and—because resistance in my case is futile—I will have probably plucked a few stems long before the harvest officially begins. Lacinato leaves should always be harvested from the base where the most mature leaves wait patiently, while shorter 'Red ruble' can be picked as needed.

As I write, I realize that I've never needed to freeze kale to store over winter, because I can always pick it fresh from the plot. Whether frost-hardened or covered by a blanket of snow, kale leaves always bounce back, and as long as you don't take too many leaves at a time, you can harvest right up until late March.

Top Harvest leaves little and often and kale will keep producing more, even through the coldest months.

Left New lacinato leaves sprout from the top, so I harvest from below, using sharp pruners.

Kitchen tip

For fresh greens in the depths of winter, I know I can rely on my favorite lacinato. I add the leaves to various dishes from lasagne to curries, and they make a fantastic spinach substitute in crispy, homemade onion bhajiyas.

SAVOY CABBAGE

Brassica oleracea (Capitata Group)

To my mind, no winter kitchen garden is complete without a row of mighty Savoy cabbages standing proud in the harshest weather. I love both the outer lush-green leaves and the paler, densely crinkled heart. When I don't need the whole head for cooking, I'll snap off just a few of the outermost leaves from one or two—a harvesting method that makes a short row of cabbages go a very long way. Compared to those of smaller, smooth-textured spring cabbages, crinkly Savoy leaves may feel a bit rubbery, but the concentration of sugars that builds up during frosty weather elevates the taste to a new level of sweetness.

Sowing and pricking out

I take a leisurely approach when sowing Savoy cabbage seed and tend to wait until the busy spring period is over. March and April see me up to my eyeballs either sowing, pricking out, or planting all the summer vegetable crops; so these seeds stay in their packet. It's only in the first half of May, when the greenhouse and cold frame are cleared

Rekha's favorites

'January King'
'Best of All'
'Vertus'

of other seedlings and I can take a break from weeding, feeding, and watering, that it's time to focus on my Savoys. I don't keep to a precise date and sow no more than 10 Savoy seeds in a seed tray of seed-starting mix at a depth of ¾in (2cm). After standing the tray in water, so that the mix gets a good soaking from the base and the seeds aren't disturbed, I put it in my north-facing cold frame out of the sun. If you don't have a cold frame, leave the seed tray on a shady windowsill.

Germination is so quick that in a couple of weeks I'm potting individual seedlings into 3½in (9cm) pots and returning them to the cold frame. Unfortunately, Savoy cabbages, like all other brassicas, are slug magnets and the pests love to munch on my emerging seedlings. So, on arrival at the plot, the very first thing I do is open the cold frame and look for slug damage. Last year I found out that slugs hate garden lime and, keen to try out this organic method of slug control, I bought a bag and sprinkled the powder around the edges of the cold frame. I had some success, although once the lime got wet I had to reapply.

Planting outside

By mid-June, when late spring gives way to early summer and flowers create pops of color among the fresh green of the plot, the Savoy seedlings have put on tremendous growth with five to six luscious green leaves per pot. Now it's time to plant them outdoors and allow the roots to

Above, left Savoy cabbage is big and blowsy, unlike the tighter heads of spring cabbage (see pp28–31).

Above In May, the greenhouse is too hot and humid for Savoy seedlings, but my north-facing cold frame is ideal.

Garden tip

As I'm planting my young Savoy cabbages, I pinch the edge of a leaf and pull gently. If a small corner comes away cleanly, it means the cabbage is well-anchored in the soil. If the whole plant comes out of the ground, the soil around the roots needs more firming in.

spread freely in the soil. I've found a calm June morning, just as the dew has evaporated, to be the best time. The soil is warm and inviting, and I'm confident there's enough moisture for the young Savoy roots to settle in well. When planting, I leave a space of 12in (30cm) between each cabbage and always firm the soil around them with my feet so they won't be rocked by strong winds when fall comes and the heads are larger. Once planting outside is complete, I water.

Unfortunately, slugs will soon track down these young Savoys, so after watering I always sink a beer trap (see p10) into the ground close by. Finally, I cover the plants with a netted cloche frame (see p168) to keep out pigeons and cabbage white butterflies (see p30).

Routine care

It's important never to let the soil around Savoy cabbages dry out. This will stress the plants and cause them to bolt (produce a flower stalk) before the heart has fully formed. In hot summer weather, especially, I water the young plants every other day. As plants establish in summer, I also feed them with my rich nettle tea (see p8). This, to be honest, smells putrid, but provides plants with a much-needed boost of nitrogen for lush green growth. I also do a weekly check for slugs, topping off the beer trap if needed, but my priority is keeping the netting secure to keep out the cabbage whites, which are desperate to lay eggs on my crop during the height of summer. Sometimes I like to stand and watch them crash into the netting. You might think me cruel, but I want to eat this vegetable—they can go lay their eggs on my horseradish leaves instead!

Harvesting

As soon as my plants have experienced an overnight frost, which improves the taste, I will harvest a few leaves as needed. A whole cabbage head is only cut from its stem if the entire family is eating together or if friends come over. Savoy cabbages are tough. They take whatever the weather throws at them, including ice and snow, and provide vitamin-rich greens over the whole winter.

Top, left Once planted, Savoys will stay in the ground for a good six months before they are ready to pick.

Right When I need a whole Savoy, I'll first inspect the leaves. After removing any damaged ones, they go straight onto the compost heap.

LEEK

Allium porrum

If I could use just one phrase to describe the leek, it would be "tough as old boots." This is a vegetable that stays in the soil for nearly a year, and gives me a good excuse to leave the warmth of my home for the freezing plot in the depths of winter. Piercing the hard, cold soil with my garden fork, I gently tease out one of the long, evergreen stems and smell its oniony aroma on the frosty air. Leeks are the easiest member of the allium (onion) family to grow and taste best when just harvested. As I walk home, all I can think of is the hearty, warming soup I'll soon be making for the family.

Sowing
Given the—frankly rubbish—weather typical of mid-February, I start the seeds off at home, sowing a small pinch of seeds (about 20) into each of two small squat pots filled with seed-starting mix and tamped down, covering them with another ½in (1cm) of sieved mix. I then stand the pots in water until the top of the mix is

Rekha's favorites

'Bleu de Solaise'
'Coloma' (heritage variety)
'Musselburgh'

moist, then move them over to a heat mat to kickstart germination. I've always sown leek seeds this way, because the seedlings won't be planted outside until late May and there is plenty of room in the pots for them to establish and grow well.

It takes about 10 days for the first seedlings to germinate, showing off a downward-dog yoga posture as they emerge (see right). As soon as this happens, I move the pots from the heat mat to the protected environment of the unheated greenhouse. The seedlings don't need to be thinned out owing to the sparse sowing, and need a drink only when the mix is dry. I water them from below as before, then let the excess drain away—leeks hate sitting in puddles.

As March begins, the seedlings are swiftly moved again, this time into the cold frame where they keep the onion and shallot seedlings company. This is the next stage in the acclimatization process before the young leeks are finally planted outdoors. Then in April, I top off the now-depleted level of nutrients in the mix by giving a rich nitrogen feed using the ratio of one measure of liquid feed to 10 parts water.

Above Long, thin leek seedlings are so flexible—as if they've been practicing yoga.

Below I gently remove the tiny seed coats that are still attached to the tips of the leek seedlings.

Planting outside

By late May, the leek seedlings are 6–8in (15–20cm) tall with thickening, sturdy stems. They're now ready to plant outdoors, but not before I've prepped the growing area. This is just as important as the seed-sowing and growing stages, and is a job I never rush. First, I rake the soil until it resembles fine crumbs, then add FBB fertilizer before raking again. If it hasn't rained the night before planting outdoors, I'll also water the planting area.

Using my dibble, I make 6in- (15cm-) deep holes in the bed at 8in (20cm) intervals. I then plant the leeks in rows, leaving 16in (40cm) between each row to improve the air flow around the plants. To make planting easier, I tend to trim off a little of the root where needed, using scissors, so the seedling fits easily into the planting hole. There's no need to back-fill. When I water, the soil naturally falls back into the hole—a process that gardeners call "dibbing in."

Routine care and pest control

Once planted, I water leeks regularly in dry weather and gently earth up the lower stems to exclude light and keep them white and tender.

Leeks, like other members of the allium family, are prone to attack by the allium leaf miner, a fly that lays its eggs close to the plants. These eggs then hatch into small grubs that burrow into the leek stem and eat through the

Above, far left Once out of the pot, I pull the clump of seedlings apart and carefully separate each one.

Left After trimming the roots to 1in (2.5cm) with scissors, the young leeks will sit at the right depth in the soil.

Center My dibble is ideal for making a row of uniform planting holes, and a stringline ensures the row is straight.

Right When I water, the soil settles loosely around the leek stems, giving them space to grow.

layers as they form. Although they don't kill the leek, the grubs certainly weaken its growth. Covering the young leeks with lightweight fleece or fine netting should stop the flies from getting in, or you can try spreading straw around the base of the plants as a deterrent.

Harvesting

Leeks are ready for harvesting from October onward. They can be left in the ground to be lifted as needed. I grow about 20 leeks, lifting just a few at a time to keep me supplied through fall and winter. If there are any plants still in the ground when spring is in full swing, they will produce flower heads that attract pollinating insects. The flowers will then set seed that you can save, store, and sow next season.

The perfect partner: Calendula

After planting the young leeks outside in May, I like to sow a few calendula (pot marigold) seeds around them. As well as brightening up the growing area with their orange blooms, the pungent scent the plants release is not a favorite among members of the fly family, including the allium leaf miner.

Above Growing alongside the crop, calendula deters leek pests and attracts pollinating insects.

Below These super-fresh leeks with clean stems are a mix of 'Lancelot' and 'Musselburgh'.

Kitchen tip

I love to use leeks as an onion substitute, and in my kitchen the leek is king during the coldest months. A hearty leek and potato soup with slivers of freshly picked kale and chunks of chorizo is a definite winter-winner in our house.

BRUSSELS SPROUTS

Brassica oleracea (Gemmifera Group)

It was my first Christmas in the UK and I had prepared sprouts for the family feast. Wow! I'd never known a vegetable to divide opinion like this. But I understand people's misgivings: back then, sprouts were often boiled to within an inch of their life, and once that smell got into your nostrils, you never forgot it. You'd think all that would be enough to put anyone off, but the sprout still makes it onto the festive dinner table.

Fortunately, modern varieties of Brussels sprouts have been bred to taste sweeter. I've also learned that they don't need to be boiled to death. But what changed my mind was growing and harvesting my own sprouts. The taste is amazing—especially after a touch of frost. Over the years, I've created delicious dishes in which my freshly picked, homegrown sprouts have had a starring role.

Sowing and repotting

I've found just two Brussels sprout plants are enough to feed my family, so there's no point in growing 20 and

Rekha's favorites

'Evesham Special'

'Kalette' (cross between sprout and kale)

'Seven Hills'

wasting seed, mix, and trays. In early April I usually sow 2–3 seeds per cell in just one row of a 1½in (4cm) cell tray at a depth of ¾in (2cm). In the spring warmth of the greenhouse, the seeds will germinate within a couple of days and grow very quickly. Within a week to 10 days, I prick out and repot the weaker seedlings to grow and donate to our allotment plant sale or give to friends, keeping the two strongest seedlings.

As the greenhouse heats up in May, I move the seedlings to my cooler, north-facing cold frame, where they won't be stressed by high temperatures. When I notice that the seedlings' roots have filled the cell, I gently squeeze from the base and the whole rootball pops out. Then I simply transplant each young Brussels sprout plant into a slightly larger 3½in (9cm) pot, water, and put them back in the cold frame.

Soil preparation and planting outside

Back in April, after sowing seeds, I dug in the green manure (see p8) that had been growing on the bed over winter, then added a bucketful of compost for a super-rich mix. After around six weeks, when I'm ready to plant the sprout seedlings outside, the organic matter will have had time to break down. This level of preparation may seem a little over the top, but as the years have gone by, I've learned that Brussels sprouts are very hungry, thirsty

Garden tip

I like to bury the young plants deeply, up to their first true leaves. I use my fists to make sure the soil around the roots is well firmed with no air pockets. This helps anchor the plants when fall and winter winds blow and the stems are heavy with budding Brussels sprouts.

Above left When pricking out spare seedlings grown in cells, I uproot them by the leaves, which are more robust than the fragile stem.

Above right To avoid accidentally knocking over and damaging the young sprouts, I set the pots on their sides before planting outside.

Above Tiny sprouts
are starting to form
at the leaf joints by
early fall.

Right Pick as many
sprouts as you plan
to eat. The rest will
keep better if left
on the plant.

Garden tip

If you haven't dug green
manure into the sprouts'
growing area, I recommend
mixing a bucketful of straw and
one of compost, and adding
this before planting outside.
Straw helps the soil hold
moisture and makes it available
to the plants' roots, especially
on hot summer days.

plants and they respond to the extra goodness and
nutrition by putting on strong, healthy growth.

At the end of May, my young plants are six or seven
weeks old—sturdy specimens with five to six true leaves.
The day before I plant them outside, I give them a good
soak, and water the planting area as well. Next morning,
while the air is cool, the soil is moist, and the plants are
well hydrated, I plant them, spacing them more closely
than the seed packets recommend—at 16in (40cm)
intervals and 6in (15cm) deep (see Garden tip, below).

Routine care

By the time the sprouts have been planted and watered,
the cabbage white butterflies are circling and determined
to find brassica leaves to lay their eggs on. As with kale
(see pp166–69), I quickly put up netting around the plants
and secure it firmly. I'll lift it every two weeks to check the
undersides of the leaves, and if I find any butterfly eggs, I
just squash them.

In the crucial growing period from mid-May to late
summer, I never let the soil around the plants dry out. By
September my efforts are rewarded when little nuggets
of Brussels sprouts begin to form where every leaf joins
the stem. It's now time to insert a stake close to each
plant, tying in the stem so that the sprout-laden stems
aren't snapped by the winds. Birds, especially pigeons, are
very keen on sprouts, so the protective netting stays on.

Harvesting

I could start picking sprouts as early as October, but I
resist and harvest my first only after an overnight frost.
This chill intensifies the sugars in the sprouts and makes
them taste sweeter. Yes—sweeter! Trust me, freshly
picked, homegrown sprouts taste far superior to any you
can buy in a store. When not much else is growing in the
plot, these plants will keep producing right up until the
end of December.

PARSNIP

Pastinaca sativa

It was only when I managed to grow parsnips successfully that I called myself a gardener. After three years of poor germination as well as poor harvests, I followed a different sowing strategy and dug in overwintering green manure (see p8) where my parsnips were to grow. This would both enrich and break up my plot's heavy clay soil. It worked! The following winter, as I carefully wiggled out and lifted long, tapering roots worthy of a prize, I let out a huge, fist-pumping "Yes!". Since then, I've grown parsnips every year. We love the taste, especially the heirloom variety 'Hollow Crown', and the distinctive aroma that fills the kitchen as they cook.

Parsnips are biennial (plants that grow in year one, then flower and die in year two), so after harvesting most of the crop, I leave a few roots in the ground. By the following midsummer, the spectacular display of yellow blooms attracts a wealth of beneficial pollinating insects to the plot. Then, once the seed heads are pale brown and ripe, I collect them to sow the following spring.

Rekha's favorites

'Gladiator'
'Hollow Crown'
'Tender and True'

Sowing and thinning

Parsnips don't need to be pampered, but they do demand some attention. I solved the poor germination problem after asking myself, "How did gardeners back in the day grow them? Did they really fuss as we do today? Of course not, they were practical people!" Soon, I found the answer: direct sowing outdoors once the soil has warmed up.

Sowing times will depend on where you live. My plot is on the outskirts of London, which means I could sow in mid- to late March for an earlier crop. But this is a busy time for me and I prefer to wait until April when the green manure has been dug in and broken down, the ground has warmed up, I've removed any stones or clods, and also raked over the soil. This is the only time you'll see me "fussing" over this vegetable.

After watering the day before, I'll sow seeds on a calm April day, making a very shallow drill with my trusty Hori Hori knife. Sowing in moist earth helps the paper-thin seeds "stick" to the soil, and I sow two or three seeds every 2in (5cm). After covering the seeds, I gently tap the row with the back of my knife to ensure they make contact with soil, then water from a can with a fine rose so the seeds aren't displaced.

Within three weeks the seedlings emerge, and I'm soon kneeling down over them. No—not praying, but carefully thinning to one seedling every 2in (5cm)! Then, at the end of May, when the remaining seedlings are outgrowing

Top Parsnip's yellow umbels not only welcome beneficial insects to the plot, but also provide me with seeds to sow next year.

Above After flowering, I wait until the seed heads look dry and collect them before the seed pods open.

Left Sowing at regular intervals, as I do with parsnip seeds, is a technique known as "station sowing."

Above Good ground preparation makes thinning parsnips easy. Here, you can see the seedlings after the row has been thinned.

Garden tip

If you haven't sown green manure in the area beforehand, I recommend growing parsnips in ground where potatoes were grown the preceding season and to which you added manure or compost. There will be enough nutrients left in the soil for the parsnips to thrive. Potatoes also help break up the soil, producing the soft, crumby texture that is perfect for sowing parsnips.

their space, I thin them again, this time removing every other plant to leave 4in (10cm) between each plant. Even at this stage, as each thinned-out parsnip is carefully removed, I can see how successfully the taproot (the part we eat) has penetrated the soft soil and grown amazingly long. Now I'm confident of a successful crop.

Routine care

Once established, parsnips are a no-fuss crop. As long as the plants are grown in full sun, watered if the soil is very dry, and weeded regularly, they will thrive over summer and produce lush rosettes of leaves. You won't need to feed them either if, like me, you have dug overwintering green manure back into the ground or planted them where potatoes were growing (see Garden tip).

Parsnips belong to the same family (Apiaceae) as carrots, and could succumb to the same well-known pest, carrot root fly (see pp36–39). The flies are attracted from far and wide by the smell of the aromatic foliage when carrot seedlings are thinned. To minimize damage by the fly's destructive grubs, I recommend never growing these two root vegetables close together.

Harvesting

By the time October arrives, my parsnips have been in the ground for six months. The leaves may look a little exhausted and have also started to turn yellow, but I know all the plants' energy has gone into producing the long, pale roots. You can begin harvesting now if you like, but I prefer to wait until November for my first harvest, and lift the roots as I need them. These hardy vegetables will come to no harm left in the ground over winter right up to March; they also taste sweeter after a frost. Before I head home, I scrub off the wet earth clinging to my freshly dug parsnips, while marveling at the length of the pale-colored roots that have spent so long underground.

Above Lift as many parsnips as you need, then leave the rest in the ground—the storage conditions are perfect

Far left I scrub the parsnips in a container of water from the butt, rather than carry the muddy roots home.

Left Time spent fussing and prepping the soil has paid off, and my reward is long, perfectly straight, white roots.

185

INDEX

A

Allium cepa 32–35, 84–87
  A. porrum 174–77
  A. sativum 100–103
  A. schoenoprasum 124–25
allium leaf miner 176–77
Anethum graveolens 116–17
aphids 98, 125
apples 138–41
  choosing the right tree 138–39
  harvesting 140
  planting trees 139–40
  routine care and pruning 140

B

basil 66, 98–99
beans, green 80–83
beets 130–33
  harvesting 132–33
  routine care 132
  sowing and thinning 130–32
Beta vulgaris 130–33
  B. v. subsp. cicla var. *flavescens* 42–45
blight 121
blood and bone meal 85
Brassica oleracea (Acephala Group) 166–69
  B. o. (Capitata Group) 28–31, 70–73
  B. o. (Gemmifera Group) 178–81
  B. o. (Italica Group) 16–19
  B. rapa (Rapifera Group) 158–61
broccoli, purple sprouting 16–19
Brussels sprouts 178–81
  harvesting 180
  routine care 180
  soil preparation and planting outside 179–80
  sowing and repotting 178–79

C

cabbages 129
  Savoy cabbage 170–73
  spring cabbage 28–31
calendula 177
Capsicum annuum 70–75, 76–79
carrot root fly 37, 38, 125
carrots 36–39
  harvesting 38
  pests 37, 38, 125, 129
  sowing 36–37
  thinning 38
celeriac 150–53
  harvesting 153
  planting outside 152, 153
  pricking out 151–52
  sowing 150–51
chard, Swiss 42–45
chiles 70–75
  growing 73–74
  harvesting 74
  sowing and repotting 71, 73
chives 124–25
cilantro 126–27
codling moths 141
companion planting 10
compost, homemade 8
Coriandrum sativum 126–27
crop rotation 11
cucumbers 60–63
  growing outdoors 61
  harvesting 62
  preparation and planting outside 61–62
  routine care 62
  sowing and hardening off 60–61
Cucumis sativus 60–63

Cucurbita moschata 154–57
  C. pepo 94–97

D

Daucus carota 36–39
dill 116–17, 153
diseases 10, 43, 102, 121

E

eggplants 56–59, 98
  growing 58–59
  harvesting 59
  sowing and repotting 56–58

F

fertilizer 8, 85
flea beetles 159–60
Florence fennel 146–49
  harvesting 148–49
  sowing 146–47
  thinning and growing 148
  watering 147
Foeniculum vulgare var. *azoricum* 146–49
Fragaria × ananassa 108–11

G

garden peas 104–107
  direct sowing and routine care 106
  harvesting 107
  planting out 105
  sowing undercover 104–105
garlic 23, 100–103
  diseases 102
  harvesting 102
  routine care 102
  sowing and planting outside 101
  types of 100–101

green beans 80–83
  harvesting and storing 82–83
  planting outside 81–82
  routine care 82
  sowing and hardening off
    80–81
green manure 8, 180, 184
gray mold 43

H
hardening off 12
herbs: basil 66, 98–99
  chives 124–25
  cilantro 126–27
  dill 116–17, 153
  mint 128–29
  parsley 46–47

K
kale 166–69
  harvesting 168
  lacinato 166, 168, 169
  preparation and planting outside
    167–68
  routine care 168
  sowing and pricking out 166–67

L
Lactuca sativa 20–23
leeks 174–77
  harvesting 177
  planting outside 176
  routine care and pest control
    176–77
  sowing 174–75
lettuce 20–23, 86
  harvesting 23
  planting outside 21–22
  sowing 20–21, 22, 23

M
Malus domestica 138–41
Mentha 128–29
mint 128–29
monthly tasks 13
moths: codling moths 141
  pea moths 106

O
Ocimum basilicum 98–99
onions 84–87
  first sowing 84–85
  growing and harvesting 86
  planting outside 85–86
  second sowing 86
  spring onions 32–35, 38
organic gardening 8–10

P
parsley 46–47
parsnips 182–85
  harvesting 184
  routine care 184
  sowing and thinning 183–84
Pastinaca sativa 182–85
pea moths 106
peas, garden 104–107
peppers, sweet 76–79
  growing 78–79
  harvesting 79
  routine care 77–78
  sowing and repotting 76–77
  watering 78
pests 10
  see also individual pests
Petroselinum crispum 46–47
Phaseolus vulgaris 80–83
pickling cucumbers 60–63

Pisum sativum 104–107
potatoes 11, 118–21, 184
  earthing up and routine
    care 120–21
  harvesting 121
  planting outside 119–20
  preparing the soil 119
  starting off seed potatoes
    118–19
  storing midseason potatoes 121
  types 119
  watering 120
purple sprouting broccoli (PSB) 16–19
  harvesting 18
  planting outside 17–18
  sowing 16–17

R
radishes 24–27
  growing and harvesting 26
  sowing outdoors 25–26
  sowing under cover 24–25
  winter radishes 26
rainwater 8
Raphanus sativus 24–27
raspberries 142–45
  choosing the variety 142–43
  harvesting 145
  planting outside 143–44
  pruning and routine
    care 144–45
Rheum × hybridum 48–51
rhubarb 48–51
  forcing and harvesting 50
  preparation and planting
    48–49
  routine care 49–50
Rubus idaeus 142–45
rust 102

S

Savoy cabbage 170–73
 harvesting 172
 planting outside 171–72
 routine care 172
 sowing and pricking out 170–71
slugs 111
Solanum lycopersicum
 64–69
 S. melongena 56–59
 S. tuberosum 118–21
spinach 112–15
 harvesting 115
 planting outside 114
 routine care 114
 sowing and container
 growing 112–13
Spinacia oleracea 112–15
spring cabbage 28–31
 harvesting 30
 planting outside 29–30
 sowing and thinning 28–29
spring onions 32–35, 38
 harvesting 34
 sowing 33–34
sprouts, Brussels 178–81
squash 154–57
 harvesting 156
 planning and sowing
 154–55
 planting outside 156
 routine care 156
strawberries 108–11
 free plants 110
 harvesting 111
 routine care 110–11
 starting off 109–10
 types 108–109
sweet corn 88–91
 harvesting 90
 planting outside 89–90
 routine care 90
 sowing 88–89

Swiss chard 42–45
 harvesting 45
 planting outside 43–45
 sowing 42–43
 thinning and hardening off 43

T

tagetes 59, 66
tomatoes 64–69
 harvesting 68
 planting outside 66–67
 routine care 67–68
 sowing and repotting
 64–65
 types of 65–66
tools, essential 12
turnips 158–61
 harvesting 160
 sowing and pest control
 158–59
 thinning and further sowings
 160

W

watering plants 8
whitefly 98

Z

Zea mays 88–91
zucchini 94–97
 harvesting 96
 preparation and planting
 outside95–96
 routine care 96
 sowing 94–95
 watering 95

ACKNOWLEDGMENTS

Picture credits

DK would like to thank Rekha
for sharing images for the
following pages: 58 (l), 65 (b),
74, 153 (r), 159(l), 177 (b).

Publisher acknowledgments

DK would like to thank Adam
Brackenbury for repro work,
Francesco Piscitelli for
proofreading and Vanessa
Bird for indexing.

Author acknowledgments

When DK, the most renowned book publisher, asked me to write with them, I somewhat ignored them! Thanks to eight weeks of patient persistence from Chris Young, AND the encouragement and loving support from the four most dear people in my life, my family, I wrote this: my first book.

My visual credits go to the amazing photographer Rachel Warne, who always requested my toes to smile through my boots (naturally, they obliged), and the careful capturing eyes of Christine Keilty. Thanks to Amy Slack for the spontaneous wiggles and jiggles just to make me smile or laugh during the long hours of photoshoot days, and also to Barbara Zuniga; one vegetable variety in my plot will forever be named 'Barbara' in her honor.

Thank you to all the companies who have supported me right from the start of my garden media journey: Spear and Jackson, Niwaki, Farmer Gracy, Haws, Woodlodge, and Overthrow Sievewrights.

A very heartfelt thank you to my wonderful allotment neighbors, Pam and Dave Marshall. You have always encouraged and supported me in every step of my gardening journey. A big huggable thanks also to Head Gardener Sean Harkin, and the whole garden team at Inner Temple Garden, for opening my eyes to another side of horticulture I've grown to love as much as kitchen gardening.

My biggest and most grateful thanks goes to my husband, Rajni, for helping me banish my self-doubts and always believing in me, and more so for patiently enduring the 20 months of this book journey with me. Ta luv x

Project Editor Amy Slack
US Editor Lori Hand
Senior Designer Barbara Zuniga
Production Editor David Almond
Production Controller Rebecca Parton
Jacket Designer Eloise Grohs
Jacket Coordinator Jasmin Lennie
Editorial Manager Ruth O'Rourke
Design Manager Marianne Markham
Art Director Max Pedliham
Publisher Katie Cowen

Editorial Anna Kruger
Design Christine Keilty
Photography Rachel Warne
Illustration Ellie Edwards Lino
Consultant Gardening Publisher Chris Young

First American Edition, 2023
Published in the United States by DK Publishing
1745 Broadway, 20th Floor, New York, NY 10019

For the curious
www.dk.com

ABOUT THE AUTHOR

Rekha Mistry is a writer and kitchen gardener, named by *Country Living* magazine as "one to watch" in 2021. After reaching the quarter-final of the BBC's *Big Allotment Challenge* in 2015, she went on to achieve an RHS Diploma in Horticulture, and in 2019 began her gardening blog, "Rekha's Garden and Kitchen." She has since written articles for magazines including *RHS The Garden, BBC Gardeners' World, Kitchen Garden*, and *Countryfile.*

To broaden her horticultural horizon, Rekha has also worked as a gardener at the historic Inner Temple Garden. Having featured her northwest London allotment on *Gardeners' World* (BBC 1) in 2020, she is now one of the show's TV hosts. She is also an Ambassador for the Heritage Seed Library, as part of her passion to protect heirloom vegetables for the future, and has more than 100,000 followers on Instagram, where her gardening adventure continues...

Instagram: **@rekha.garden.kitchen**
Facebook: **Rekha's Garden & Kitchen**

For more information about Rekha, or to discover her recipes (including her famous rhubarb cake, see p51), head to: **rekhagardenkitchen.com.**

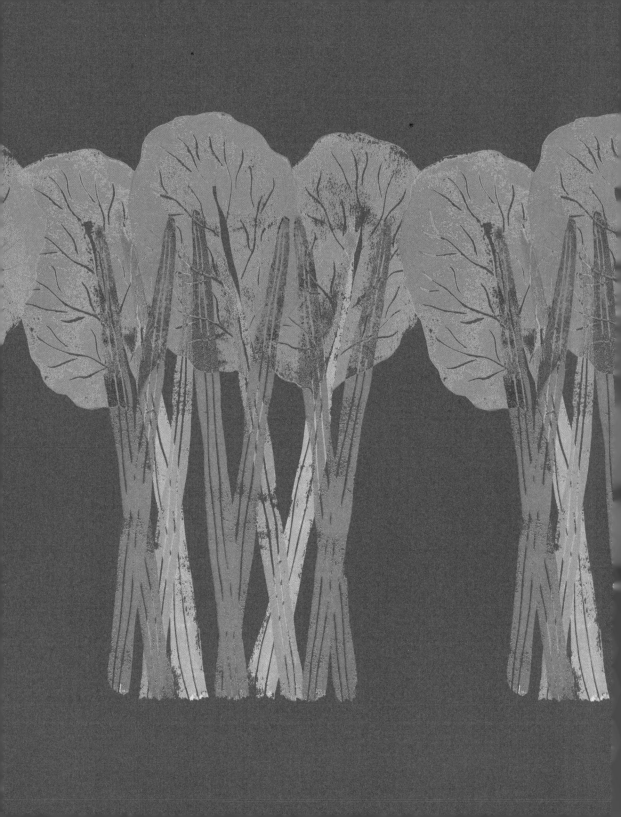